July 24.
OKE HAMPTON.
Book shop.

Mary Bell
Hurle House
Hatherleigh.

If this book should chance to roam; read it,
enjoy it then send it home. MR Bell.

• HALSGROVE DISCOVER SERIES ➤

DARTMOOR

WALKS INTO HISTORY

JOHN EARLE

HALSGROVE

First published in Great Britain in 2003

British Library Cataloguing-in-Publication Data
A CIP record for this title is available from the British Library

ISBN 1 84114 256 5

HALSGROVE

Halsgrove House
Lower Moor Way
Tiverton, Devon EX16 6SS
Tel: 01884 243242
Fax: 01884 243325
email: sales@halsgrove.com
website: www.halsgrove.com

Printed by D'Auria Industrie Grafiche Spa, Italy

CONTENTS

DARTMOOR NATIONAL PARK

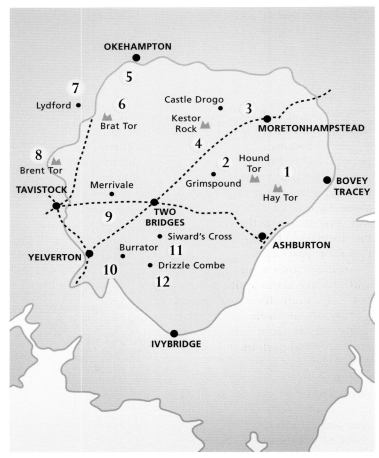

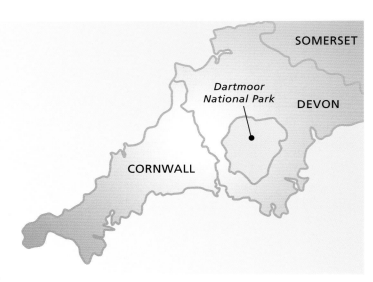

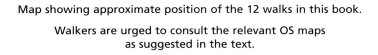

Map showing approximate position of the 12 walks in this book.

Walkers are urged to consult the relevant OS maps as suggested in the text.

INTRODUCTION

One would be hard pushed to find another area in Britain that had such marvellous walking country and that was as rich in historic sites, from prehistoric times right up to the present, as Dartmoor. I find the history of man on Dartmoor, especially the prehistoric period, absorbing and fascinating. I still feel a strange prickling sensation in my scalp when I am alone in one of the areas of hut circles or stone rows; I can almost sense the spirits of the Bronze-Age people of four thousand years ago.

In this book I shall be visiting and writing about quite a number of prehistoric sites on Dartmoor, as well as a great many others from the Norman and medieval periods through to recent historic times.

But what of the walking? I have lived for over sixty years near or on Dartmoor and have also walked and climbed in many areas of the world such as the

A clapper bridge on the River Avon.

Himalayas, Tierra del Fuego, and Baffin Island, but I still find Dartmoor a most exciting, interesting and intriguing corner of our varied world. It has been called the last great wilderness in southern England and is, indeed, a huge, largely uninhabited, lonely area of moorland of some 365 square miles. This is one reason why I find Dartmoor so attractive and I hope you will too. I love the wild, lonely, remote areas of uplands and mountains. Even at crowded holiday periods you can still get away from the masses and walk all day without seeing a soul.

Dartmoor has a fresh, indefinable scent that changes with the seasons. Sometimes the misty air is full of the smell of damp, peaty moorland, at others the pungent scent of gorse. In March when the farmers are swaling (burning the moor to improve the grass for grazing) the wind brings a waft of the burnt heather and gorse or a smell of the smoke itself.

The rolling horizon of Dartmoor with its huge skies always thrills me. Except in a few steep-sided valleys you are never shut in on the moor; you always have a feeling of distance and vast open spaces. Everywhere, unless there has been a prolonged summer drought, there is the presence of water; quaking bogs, small streams and peaty, moorland rivers tumbling down over water-rounded boulders while high overhead the skylarks pour out their own evocative liquid song.

As we shall see a lot of the landscape, certainly on the margins where early man farmed and in some of the remote river valleys where the old tinners worked, has been fashioned and changed by humans. Man has lived, hunted and worked on Dartmoor since prehistoric times and has obviously left his mark, from hut circles, stone rows and megaliths, to tinners' spoil tips and blowing houses, to newtakes, peat cuttings and ancient field systems, to china-clay works, forestry plantations, dams and even, controversially, a modern bypass around Okehampton. I shall be writing about many of the above as we walk out to look at the sites, but if you require further information on these subjects, I recommend you refer to the DNPA's revised edition of *Archaeology of the Dartmoor Landscape*.

So what of man today? Sadly there are very few of the true, old Dartmoor farmers and their families left in our modern times. These were men and women for whom a trip to Exeter or Plymouth was a once-a-year outing, who thought nothing of travelling to market in a gig or cart taking two or three hours there and back again, whose slow hard life revolved round the seasons and the harsh taskmaster, Dartmoor. Life is still hard and uncertain for Dartmoor farmers but for entirely different and often frustrating reasons.

Many things have changed from the days when every small village had its bakery and blacksmith, when the grocer, the butcher, even the fishmonger from Brixham, the haberdasher and the tailor delivered to the door of remote farms

Black Tor Fall, close to Burrator Reservoir.

by pony and trap, when harvest suppers and whortleberry-gathering parties, with whole villages going on to the moor, were part of the years' major social events. But here and there are a few folk whose memories reach back to the way of life adopted by their forefathers; a way of life that has gone forever.

During these walks you will come in contact with some of the wildlife of Dartmoor. The buzzard, with its moth-like wings and mewing call, is the most common big bird on the moor and in many ways epitomises Dartmoor with its soaring freedom, or like a sentinel sitting on a pole or bare tree surveying the world. You might also get a glimpse of a hill fox loping off to steal a chicken or kill a new-born lamb. It is the skylark, that minute speck in the blue summer sky, with its bubbling song, that brings back a surge of happy childhood memories of walking or riding on hot breathless days into the heart of the moor. Even now I still scan the sweeping skies trying to find the little, soaring creature pouring out its ecstasy.

Through this guide, my aim is to share with you some of the magic and mystery of the history of Dartmoor and the delight of walking there. I will show you places to visit that I hope will interest and fascinate you, so that like me you will become a person who loves and appreciates this lonely wilderness and will return to it again and again, for it has a haunting, almost hypnotic influence on all who walk there.

John Earle, 2003.

WALKS INTO HISTORY

You should be able to walk some 4kph on most walks but it is best to allow at least ten minutes in every hour to rest, look around, study maps and explore the various points of interest. Be sure to have warm clothing, a really good, comfortable pair of boots, waterproofs and something with which to cover your head if it rains. A small rucksack is useful to carry spare clothing, food for the day, a water bottle or Thermos and a small first-aid kit.

MAPS AND COMPASSES

It does not take long to master elementary map reading, which is all you need to successfully follow the routes in this guide. There are three different scales of maps that you will come across and are likely to use. Firstly there is the Ordnance Survey's Landranger Series on Dartmoor which uses a scale of 2cm to 1km (1:50 000) or about 1.25 inches to the mile. You will need two sheets for the whole of Dartmoor: Sheet 191 covers Okehampton and North Dartmoor while Sheet 202 covers Torbay and South Dartmoor. The Ordnance Survey also produces perhaps the best map of Dartmoor for detail – the Outdoor Leisure Series, Sheet 28, better known as the Explorer Series. The scale is 4cm to 1km (1:25 000) or 2.50 inches to the mile. It covers the whole of Dartmoor (although please note Walk 8 is not covered on this map) with superb detail. However it is a huge sheet, printed on both sides and the problems of folding and making visible the section that you want to use are hysterical on windy, rainy days! If you are not careful you may take off like a hang-glider! The saving grace is that you can buy waterproofed, laminated copies of the map.

The clapper bridge at Postbridge.

Finally Harvey Map Services Ltd have made two excellent maps of Dartmoor in their Walkers Maps Series. Again there are two of them, North and South Dartmoor, and they are both waterproof. They are a scale of 2.5cm to 1km (1:40 000) and use an orienteering map style of presentation with different colours to indicate different vegetation and conventional signs that show many details of the landscape. Therefore the physical features of the moor are all important, but the place-names shown are limited. One useful feature is that the maps show the marshy areas very clearly; important information when on Dartmoor! The result is a clear, uncluttered map that I find very easy to use.

There is one important feature of maps that I need to make sure you understand so you must forgive me if you already know about grid lines. I use what are called grid references to pin-point exactly the starting-point of each walk as well as other features to which I may want to refer. The parallel lines printed on all the maps, that I have mentioned above, are the grid lines. Each line has a number to identify it. The numbers of the lines that run up and down the sheet increase as they move towards the right or east and these lines are called eastings. The ones that run across the map increase as they move up the sheet or north. They are called northings. Each square created by the grid lines is 1km by 1km. The diagonal across the square from corner to corner is 1.5km. This is a very easy way to estimate distance. Regardless of the scale of the map the grid squares are always 1km by 1km. Obviously the larger the scale of the map the larger the square will be on the map.

Perhaps the most important use of the grid lines is to enable the use of grid (or map) references; the numbers of the eastings are always given first, followed by the northings. To give the position of a large area, such as a village, you need to give a four-figure reference which would indicate just the square (e.g. the village of Holne lies in the square 70 eastings and 69 northings – in other words SX7069). However it is customary to give a six-figure reference and to do this you need to subdivide each square into tenths. You give the main number of the eastings square, followed by the tenths eastward, followed by the main northings square and finally the tenths northward, e.g. the reference for Dartmeet would be 672 eastings and 732 northings, given as just SX672732. However you must remember that a six-figure reference gives you a square that is 100m by 100m on the ground and that is a fairly large area if you are looking for a small feature. It is possible, obviously, to give eight figure references which covers a square 10m by 10m but it is quite difficult to do this with any accuracy.

Bowerman's Nose.

You may wonder to what the SX refers. As similar references occur every 100km you should always prefix your grid reference with the grid letters which refer uniquely to one area of the British Isles. For Dartmoor these letters are SX. As I am obviously referring only to Dartmoor within this guide, I shall not prefix all my map references with SX.

You will need a proper navigating compass as the small button compasses are not really of any use. It should have a clear plastic base with a swivelling capsule and a luminous needle (you need to be able to use it in mist or poor visibility).

Approaching Chalk Ford.

WHERE TO STAY

There is a vast array of accommodation across Dartmoor – ranging from the large and expensive to the small and not so expensive. As you drive across the moor you will often see farms and small guest-houses advertising B&Bs, camping barns and bunkhouses, as well as hotels and youth hostels. You may be the sort of person who likes to try places on the off-chance that they will have vacancies, but at peak holiday periods you would probably benefit from booking in advance.

USING THE GUIDE

These walks are more or less in an anticlockwise circle starting from my home near Widecombe-in-the-Moor and ending up south of the moor. I have assumed that you will be travelling by car, so most of the walks are circular. However the Dartmoor National Park Authority is keen to keep down the numbers of people who use their cars on Dartmoor. If you decide to venture out without your vehicle, public transport is available; Dartmoor's traveline is always useful: 0870 608 2608.

Crockern Tor; the tinners' parliament.

I have graded all the walks in the book firstly by length: long: 7.5 miles (12km) or more; medium: 2.5 miles (4km) to 7.5 miles (12km); short: under 2.5 miles (4km). Secondly I have classed the walks hard, moderate or easy, depending on the difficulty of the terrain, the climbing involved and the map reading and navigation skills you will need to employ. With the last, however, it is certainly wise to remember that what may be easy on a clear, sunny day may actually be pretty tricky if the mists come down or the weather deteriorates.

A burial cairn on Rippon Tor.

I refer to lefts and rights as if you are following the correct direction of travel. However, I refer to the true left and right banks of streams and rivers; in other words, as if you are looking downstream.

Do not forget to check the firing notices for any walks on the North Moor that might take you into the ranges (see local newspapers on Fridays, contact information centres or use the freephone number: 0800 458 4868).

I have not given the time that I think the walk will take – you will need to work it out for yourselves depending on the fitness of your party and whether you want to wander gently along, exploring and looking as you go. I hope that this book encourages just that.

I suppose what I am suggesting is that you might like to use this guide as a basis for walks that you can work out for yourselves rather than following slavishly the exact routes I have described (although obviously I hope you will follow some of my walks as they are all ones that I have enjoyed over the years).

Finally I hope that some of you who cannot walk or may not want to walk will also be able to use this guide so that, with the aid of a map and what I have written, you will be able to come with me on some of the walks in your imagination, and find out more about Dartmoor, this extraordinary and fascinating place, that is so steeped in history.

WALK 1

SADDLE TOR, LOW MAN, HAY TOR, HAYTOR QUARRIES, THE GRANITE RAILWAY, HOLWELL QUARRIES, GREATOR ROCKS, MEDIEVAL VILLAGE, HOUND TOR, BONEHILL ROCKS, TOP TOR, PIL TOR, FOALE'S ARRISHES.

**START: Car park near Saddle Tor. Map ref.: 749762.
Long: 7.75 miles/12.5km. Moderate.**

You could start at the popular Hay Tor car park along the road but this one below Saddle Tor is far less busy. Widecombe-in-the-Moor is 3.5km away with all the facilities of a popular, tourist village. Bovey Tracey is 8km away and is a small town, which offers all the facilities you might require. There are ice-cream and snack vans situated at the Hay Tor car parks in summer and there is a Dartmoor National Park information caravan at the lower Hay Tor car park.

This is quite a long walk but it can certainly be cut short or even done in separate sections. For example, you could include just the Haytor Quarries from the Saddle Tor start. Alternatively you could take in the Hound Tor and the Saxon-village part of the walk by starting at the car park at Hound Tor, (map ref.: 739792) and going out to the village and back again. There is an ice-cream van here too during summer and some weekends.

From the car park at **Saddle Tor** set off up the path north-east that leads to the col between the two summits. From there you will see the huge rock-face of Low Man across a stretch of moorland about 1km away. When you reach it you will appreciate its size for it is the largest natural rock-face on Dartmoor. There are some excellent and extremely severe rock climbs on it, some of which are over 150ft, but one of the less hair-raising ones, called Raven's Gully goes up the obvious gully on the left of the face.

Walk round to the left below **Low Man** and then, if you wish to go easily to the top, scramble further round and you will find some steps cut into the granite

Hay Tor (left) *and Low Man, seen from Saddle Tor.*

11

Low Man.

Water lilies and a wooden beam at Haytor Quarries.

with an iron handrail and rungs on the south-east side of the tor overlooking the car park.

The names on Dartmoor can be confusing and Hay Tor is a classic example. It is, of course, High Tor, which in the vernacular becomes Heytor. The Ordnance Survey, however, uses the modern (and incorrect) transcription, Hay Tor. The other confusion is that if you talk about the rock itself, it is Hay Tor, but if you refer to the Quarries or the Down, it becomes Haytor (e.g. Haytor Quarries). There are many more such bewildering examples to be found on Dartmoor!

Across a little grassy bay you will see **Hay Tor** itself. There are many good rock climbs on this tor too but, again, if you wish to get easily to the top there is a flight of steps cut into the granite that start on the east side. These steps caused the considerable indignant wrath of a certain Dr Crocker who denounced them in 1851 as 'the unsightly stair step to enable the enervated and pinguedinous scions of humanity of this wonderful nineteenth century to gain its summit'. I wonder what he would think of the hordes today who stagger to the top. However, standing as they do on the south-eastern edge of Dartmoor, the views from both these tors are magnificent. Looking south to the coast with Torbay and Lyme Bay visible, you can just see part of the Teign estuary. Below you are the flat areas of the Bovey Beds where there is a thriving china-clay industry that utilises decomposed granite eroded and washed off Dartmoor. To the east you can see Haldon Hill outside Exeter with its folly tower of Lawrence Castle or Haldon Belvedere. Northwards you look over the eastern edge of the moor up to Cawsands Beacon or Cosdon Hill on the northern limits of Dartmoor. All around to the north-west, west and south-west you can see the rolling moor stretching far away with, in summer, skylarks trilling overhead. It is no wonder that this is a popular place, so if you prefer quiet and solitude do not come here at peak holidays times or fine weekends!

From the east side of Hay Tor you will see a path running down the hill towards the north-east to some granite spoil tips. When you get closer to the mounds of waste you can make out a wire fence around a quarry. There is a gate at the far, eastern end where a track comes up from the south-east and the lower Hay Tor car park. Go into the **quarry** by the gate and you will find your-self in an unexpected, magical place where man has destroyed large areas of the natural environment but where nature has taken over again. When man has gone, nature returns the land to something beautiful, unexpected and unusual. Heather and gorse grow in profusion on the once-harsh rock-faces whilst in summer dragonflies and butterflies flit over the man-made pools where water lilies grow. Trees and reeds have seeded themselves on the edges of the deep flooded pits.

You are looking at the remains of part of one of Dartmoor's extraordinary industrial enterprises whose opening was described on 16 September 1820 in the *Exeter Flying Post* as follows:

On Saturday Mr George Templer, of Stover House, gave a grand fête champêtre on Haytor Down, on the completion of the granite railroad. The company assembled at its foot on Bovey Heathfield, and in procession passed over it to the rock. A long string of carriages, filled with elegant and beautiful females, multitudes of horse-men, workmen on foot, the wagons covered with laurels and waving streamers, formed in their windings through the valley an attractive scene to spectators on the adjacent hill. Old Haytor seemed alive; its sides were lined with groups of persons, and on its top a proud flag fluttered in the wind. Previously to returning to dine, Mr George Templer addressed the assemblage in a short and energetic speech, which excited bursts of applause. He stated the causes that induced him to engage in such a great undertaking. He pointed out the advantages which it offered to the sur-rounding proprietors, the employment it would find for the mechanic and labourer, and its tendency to increase in a great degree the trade of the port of Teignmouth. In adverting to the Plymouth Railway, he expressed his hope that both might prosper, and not endanger, by improper rivalry, the success of either.

The Rock Inn, Haytor, 1896. This is one of a number of dwellings built in Haytor Vale by George Templer for his quarry workers.

The Templer family had lived for three generations at Stover House and it was the father, James Templer, who had built the Stover Canal from Newton Abbot to Teigngrace. Quite clearly they were an enterprising family and it was the son, George, who conceived the idea of linking the end of his father's canal with the quarries at Haytor and Holwell, that were already operating, by a tramway. George was quite a lad who was well known for being something of a scholar as well as for his prowess in the hunting field. As can be seen in his speech reported above he felt strongly about providing employment for local people and helping the economy of the county and local towns such as Teignmouth.

There must have been a major incentive to get the granite down to Teignmouth to be exported by sea. Indeed, there was the possibility of a con-tract to provide granite for the new London Bridge and eventually for a great many other buildings in London.

Granite rails at Haytor Quarries.

The name of the engineer who designed the tramway is not known but the idea to use granite instead of iron rails was brilliant. The granite was already being extracted from the quarries at Haytor and Holwell. Importantly, the product was cheap. It was also a type of granite that was able to resist pressure. This is an example of Dartmoor granite being used for the most extraordinary and unlikely objects.

The rails were hewn of various lengths with a 3in. flange and a gauge of 4ft 3in. They even had points that worked by having metal cheek-pieces pivoting on a peg, with a socket in the junction stone.

The cut blocks of granite for export were carried on huge, flat, wooden trucks with gravity acting as the power for the journey off the moor as they set off in trains of 12. It must have been a hair-raising, hazardous business as the trucks only had a primitive device for a brake – a wooden pole that a wretched driver had to apply manually to the rim of the wheels, which ran loose on their axles. I cannot find any accounts of accidents but they must have occurred! For the upward journey from Teigngrace, detachable shafts were fitted and teams of as many as 18 horses began the long slog back up to Hay Tor. A local jingle ran:

Drilled grooves for the iron wedges that split the granite.

Eighteen brave steed and twelve old car
To take stone from Ovals Tor;
The stallion in front they did place
It was John Murrin's of Teigngrace.

Apparently John Murrin belonged to a family that ran the stables where the horses where kept as well as a smithy, for shoeing the horses, I presume. With an eye to the main chance, they also owned an inn. All these businesses were at Ventiford Wharf which was where the granite tramway met the terminal basin of the Stover Canal near Teigngrace.

When you walk into the quarry you will see between the two pools at the west end an old wooden beam and an iron winch, which are the remnants of a crane that once hoisted blocks of granite onto the trucks.

Go back now out through the gate again and work your way through the huge mounds of waste towards the east. The grassy area you will see was where small huts, homes to the quarrymen, once stood. They were good enough for the early days but as business increased for The Haytor Granite Company George Templer realised that he needed a larger workforce and that his workers needed more comfortable houses, especially those with families, so he built some cottages at Haytor Vale nearby. Two families lived in each cottage. Their rent was either 6d. (2.5p in modern money) or 1s.3d. (about 7p) per week, depending whether they lived in the front or the back part of the cottage. Nearly 100 men worked at the quarry at the height of its production and some had to walk up to work from Widecombe-in-the-Moor, Manaton, Ilsington and even Bovey Tracey. Imagine walking for an hour or more to spend the day at hard, manual work and then walking back again at the end of the day.

Haytor Quarries.

Keep walking east and you soon come to the quite remarkable **granite rails** of the tramway. They are still clearly visible and look almost as if you could run trucks on them even now, after nearly two hundred years.

George Templer got the contract for the granite for London Bridge in 1825 and more contracts followed. The sudden increase in loading granite at the old quay at Teignmouth Docks began to cause problems, so by 1826 New Quay was built and hundreds of tons of Dartmoor granite were shipped from Teignmouth up the English Channel, round into the Thames and into the heart of the City of London.

A Mr Bigg who was the London agent and secretary of the Haytor Granite Company wrote often to George Templer explaining that the Dartmoor quarries were in harsh competition with quarries in Aberdeen and Peterhead and even more so with Penryn in Cornwall where it was easier to get the granite to the ships for export. Bigg was justly proud of the list of buildings, including that first contract for the new London Bridge, that did in fact use Dartmoor granite. He wrote:

The Company feel a proud satisfaction in stating that Haytor Granite has been entirely used in the New Goldsmiths' Hall; New Fishmongers' Hall; Ramsgate Harbour Monument; Shoreham Bridge; Christ's Hospital; King's College; Waithman's Obelisk; Pitt's pedestal in Hanover Square; George the Fourth's pedestal in Edinburgh; and the pedestal for the equestrian Statue in Windsor Park; whilst a large proportion of Haytor has been used in the Covent Garden and Hungerford Markets; Westminster; New Bridewell; Custom House; Buckingham Palace, etc.

To this list he might have added Tothill Fields Prison and the magnificent polished columns, of a single block each, in the library of George IV at the British Museum.

All these contracts from 1825–35 were the highlights of the industry and indeed justified the building of the tramway but it became more difficult for Bigg to get trade and demand fell away in the 1840s and '50s. In 1858 the tramway was closed as the competition from Penryn proved too much.

By the 1880s Haytor and Holwell Quarries were disused. However in 1919 a great block of granite was cut from Haytor Quarries to be used for the Exeter War Memorial. It was carried away by traction-engine and trailer and took twice as long as it might have done in the days of George Templer's granite railway! It was the end of a remarkable era.

If you look at the 1:25 000 map you will see marked The Templer Way. This follows the line of the old tramway, often with the granite rails visible, especially beside the road near Brimley, all the way off the moor down to

Haytor Quarries, now reclaimed by nature.

Teigngrace. It is a fascinating walk to follow and it certainly makes you appreciate what an extraordinary feat of engineering and inspiration the tramway represents.

Back now to our walk. If you went out to the east to find the granite rails you need to follow them round quite a way to the west until you come to some points and here you must take the right-hand track downhill. You will see ahead of you a jumble of waste mounds below Holwell Tor. Follow the rails over more points and you will soon be in **Holwell Quarries**.

Holwell Quarries, from a nineteenth-century print.

Again there are quite a few interesting things to be seen here. An amazing, sheer, smooth rock-face is hidden just around the corner. You will pass several small, ruined buildings where stonemasons and blacksmiths would have worked. There are several sections of the granite rail that run at right angles to and across the main track. These rails took the trucks out on to the jetties of rock facing north for dumping waste material.

If you keep walking past the main quarries, where the track begins to swing round to the left, look down to a small platform some 15ft or so below you on your right and you will see a small, stone, beehive-shaped hut with a low entrance. It has been suggested that this was built as a shelter for the quarrymen to use when they were blasting. It is still in remarkable condition but sadly over the past few years it has begun to deteriorate helped, I am sure, by vandals. As with the Haytor Quarries this is a place of ghosts and deserted memories, that nature has gradually reclaimed.

Spoil tips at Holwell Quarries with Greator Rocks and Hound Tor beyond.

Retrace your steps back past the quarries and start to climb up the hill the way you came down the track. After 150yds or so you will see a path on your left that contours around the head of the marshy valley of the side stream of the Becka Brook. Follow this path, that will be deep in bracken in the summer, to Smallacombe Rocks. There are some hut circles on the flank of the tor, on your right.

You may have to find your own way down north-west from the rocks. There is a path but it is quite hard to find. However at the bottom you should find the track that runs through a mass of boulders into the woods and eventually on 'the right of way' over a stone bridge that crosses the Becka Brook after it has flowed out of the lakes, made by damming the stream. This is a delightful valley owned by the Leighon Estate but a lot of it is private land.

Quarrymen's hut below Holwell Quarries.

*Greator Rocks and Hound Tor
from Holwell Quarries.*

After the little stone bridge there is a steep climb which will take you past **Greator Rocks** that you will have seen from the opposite side of the valley. They form a long and impressive rock-face seen from the east although, surprisingly, there are only a few rock climbs here. If you are feeling agile you might like to do a scrambling traverse of the ridge of Greator Rocks. The views are splendid to the east, with the valley clothed with bluebells looking like a blue mist, in May and June, falling away to the lakes below and with Holwell Tor, Hay Tor and Low Man lining the hill opposite. You could almost imagine you were in the high mountains here; Crib Goch, Striding Edge and even the Alps when there is snow about!

Follow one of the tracks to the ruins you will see on your right, with Hound Tor, which now dominates the skyline, looming beyond to the north-west. As you walk towards the low ruins, you will see that the whole area of the wide, flat valley of Houndtor Down has a great many banks and walls – remnants of ancient field systems. A corn ditch, (a deep-walled ditch) to keep the deer out, has been identified. You are now on the site of a ***medieval village*** mentioned in the Domesday Book as the Manor of Hundatora, linked with the abbey at

Left: *Remains of the medieval village of Hundatora.*

Above: *A fireplace and oven in the medieval village.*

Tavistock. It was the subject of intense archaeological excavations and digs in the 1960s under the guidance of Lady Aileen Fox, the well-known archaeologist, responsible for many of the digs on Dartmoor in the 1950s and '60s. A great many interesting insights into how people lived and worked in the tenth to fourteenth centuries were discovered; often, the remains of a new dwelling was built on the foundations of an earlier one.

The site of a settlement was all important and it is easy to see why this particular venue was chosen. It had to be sheltered from the prevailing winds and bad weather and there had to be a good supply of water nearby. It was also vital that there was level land for the fields and good grazing for the stock. This whole area had been inhabited by Bronze-Age people and it is interesting to note that it was during the medieval period that man changed from building round huts to rectangular houses, surprisingly made of wattle and turf. Why he rejected the granite lying all around nobody is quite sure.

What you can see here are probably the main foundations and low walls on top of which wattle partitions were built. The roofs were thatched probably with turf or heather and later the straw from rye and broom. Archaeologists discovered houses and barns, some with fireplaces and ovens, which can still be seen today, that were used for drying the corn grown in the wet Dartmoor fields surrounding the village. There is also one building that has an entrance passage with the remains of an alcove in it, facing north-east to avoid the sun and probably to keep food cool. This may have been somewhere families could sit on hot summer days. These were the beginnings of the longhouses that later became the traditional style for Dartmoor farmhouses, many of which are still standing today.

From the way the ruins are set out it is possible to see the how the 'pecking order' of society was determined. There is obviously one large manor-house where the lord lived. In addition there are three longhouses for his villeins, with, as was the case until quite recent times, byres for the cattle at one end of the longhouse. Both humans and animals entered the building through one large entrance. Finally there are three small one-roomed cottages.

It has been suggested that it was the Black Death, in 1348, that caused such villages to be abandoned as whole communities died of the plague. (There is another similar village, Hutholes, situated close to my home near Widecombe-in-the-Moor.) Hundatora is a fascinating place in a most beautiful setting.

Strike up the hill now towards *Hound Tor*. This, I think, is my favourite tor with its two wide, grassy avenues running through towering granite walls on either side. Here you will find great blocks of rock, pillars, cracks and small caves all covering a large area where you could spend a long time scrambling and exploring. From some angles it looks like a ruined castle or some great creature crouching on the hill. The name comes from the fact that one rock is said to look like a hound's head while others say that the tor looks like the Bowerman's pack of hounds turned to stone by the witches. By the way the Bowerman's Nose is just down the road! Finally, there are some fine rock climbs here.

The views looking back to Greator Rocks and Hay Tor are impressive while, away to the north, from the top of the highest point, you can look along the eastern edge of Dartmoor, past Chagford to Cosdon Hill, also known as Cawsands Beacon.

Walk south now from Hound Tor and divert to have a look at the remaining cairn circle and kistvaen on the open land opposite the drive to Hedge Barton.

Hay Tor and Low Man seen from Hound Tor.

Sections of the kist are missing, having been taken, it is said, when the roads were constructed.

Aim south to the edge of the open moor where a wall will lead you down to the road. Walk for a short distance along the road and you soon come to a cattle-grid. After the grid, it is best to walk across the moorland to your left rather than out across a rather wet and marshy area close to the wall.

Straight ahead is the line of Bell Tor and Chinkwell Top. You should aim more or less straight at **Bonehill Rocks** to the left. These rocks are also worth exploring if you have time and the views over the Widecombe valley are superb. You may see climbers here as they use it for 'bouldering', a sort of rock-climbers' gymnasium!

Aim south again across the open moorland to the top of Widecombe Hill where you cross over the road and walk to **Top Tor**. From here you will see the low banks and walls of your next point, **Foale's Arrishes**, south-east of **Pil Tor**. You must not wander too far to your right as you drop down towards Foale's Arrishes as it is pretty marshy in Blackslade Mires.

You can find history from the Bronze Age up to fairly recent times in this one locality. In various excavations eight double-walled Bronze-Age huts were discovered all between 18ft and 30ft in diameter, some with sleeping platforms. One of the larger huts had a paved and curved annexe jutting out from the wall in which was found charcoal and bits of pottery. This space was probably a kitchen. Other interesting objects found here were scrapers used for smoothing arrowheads. However, it seems that occupation must have been over many centuries; pottery found in different shapes and with varying ornamentation indicates that Iron-Age people must have taken over the site. This is interesting as there are very few Iron-Age remains on Dartmoor. We shall visit one of the other sites in a later walk. There is evidence therefore of occupation from 1200BC until around 400BC.

The remains of Newhouse, the inn at Foale's Arrishes.

The remains of old Bronze-Age and Iron-Age field boundaries ('Celtic field systems') indicate that both groups were farmers. However, much has been lost as a result of medieval and later-nineteenth-century activities.

Walk across to the road and on the far side you will see a flat rock with 'A' carved on it with the date 1793. This is one of the boundary stones of the parish of Ashburton.

On the west side of the road there are a number of low walls, some thorn trees and a pleasant grassy yard. This is all that remains of Newhouse, a pub that was burnt down a great many years ago. It stood at an important crossing place with roads leading to Ashburton, Moretonhampstead, Bovey Tracey and Chagford. It was visited by travellers using the bleak, moorland road who were probably in the tin trade (both Ashburton and Chagford were stannary towns) but especially by men who drove wagons carrying wool to the woollen industry that thrived in Chagford, and lime for the fields in that area. Apparently these men would drive like mad to get to the kilns early in order to avoid waiting. They would then get rid of their loads of lime, tin or wool as quickly as possible before setting off for home, spending the rest of the day in this pub on the return journey! A large number of carts with patiently waiting horses could be seen lining the road near this lonely inn while gallons of cider and ale went down the throats of the drivers! Happy days! Plus ça change!

The last landlord of Newhouse was a man called Foale and it's his arrishes that you can see. The word 'arrish' is Devon slang for field. Obviously Foale did not make the walls of the fields as they were already there from the Bronze- and Iron-Age days but he utilised the prehistoric enclosures for his stock and probably added to them, so it is his name that has remained.

There is one final strange story that was told of how a local man boasted, much to the dismay of his neighbours, that he would build a house and farm within these ancient banks, reaves and huts and spend the rest of his days there. However one day he suddenly disappeared and was never seen again. Was it the pixies or the ghosts of the Bronze- and Iron-Age people who spirited him away, or just another Dartmoor legend?

The church at Widecombe-in-the-Moor.

Walk along the side of the road to the junction at Hemsworthy Gate to an area called Seven Lords Lands. Just north, along the road towards Widecombe-in-the-Moor and quite close to the wall on the right, there is a fine, large, stone circle which is said to be the boundary marker of seven manors – hence the name Seven Lords Lands. A short walk along the road east after the cattle-grid or on the verge on either side of the road will take you past several gullies or small gerts from a disused mine and soon you will be back at the car park below Saddle Tor.

George French, who assisted on a number of early archaeological excavations on Dartmoor, seen here at Foale's Arrishes, 1896.

WALK 2

GRIMSPOUND, HOOKNEY TOR, HEADLAND WARREN FARM, CHALLACOMBE STONE ROW, VITIFER AND BIRCH TOR MINES, GOLDEN DAGGER MINE, THE MEDIEVAL VILLAGE OF CHALLACOMBE.

**START. Lay-by beside the road below Grimspound.
Map ref.: 697809. Medium. 5 miles/8km. Moderate.**

If there are no places here for your car, as it can be busy, then park in a small quarry a short distance up the road on your right.

There are no facilities close to this start except perhaps the Warren House Inn (map ref.: 675809) on the main road across the moor from Moretonhampstead to Postbridge and Two Bridges. The Warren House Inn is said to be the third highest pub in Britain and obviously as its name suggests it was a place where the landlords also used to breed rabbits on a commercial basis keeping them in man-made burrows. Like the ruins of the inn on the Ashburton to Chagford road (Walk 1) the Warren House Inn was also known as Newhouse and was originally on the opposite side of the road – it is still possible to see the foundations. It was a popular drinking haunt of the men who worked in the various mines that you will visit on this walk. It is said that the fire, which used to burn peat, has not been extinguished for a century. I leave you to believe this yarn or not.

The other story told about the Warren House Inn also needs some believing but the same tale occurs in various other parts of Dartmoor and indeed was recounted by Henry Williamson, the author of *Tarka the Otter*, in one of his short stories. As such, I am inclined to believe it.

One stormy night the snowdrifts around the Warren House Inn were so deep that a traveller going across the moor was forced to ask for a bed and lodging there. He was received with great hospitality and after a good meal he was

The Warren House Inn.

shown to his bedroom. In the corner was a great chest and overcome with curiosity he peeped inside. You can imagine his horror when he saw, laid out in it, the body of an old man. He spent a sleepless night, cowering at every creak and groan in the old house, thinking that the owners were murderers who killed their guests for money and disposed of the bodies claiming later that the missing person must have got lost on the moor. However, in the morning, pale, weary and with great trepidation, he plucked up enough courage to ask about the body in the chest. 'Why bless you,' said the landlady. She continued:

That's father. He died a few weeks back and what with the weather being so bad and the ground frozen so hard, we have not been able to bury him, so we salted him down as we do with the bacon! When the weather improves we shall take him along to Widecombe to bury him!

You may or may not like to call at the Warren House Inn, as you get quite close to it about halfway round this walk!

Set off up the track that runs up the hill towards the east beside a small brook running over rocks and sometimes in deep gullies. It won't be long before you come to the outer wall of **Grimspound**, one of the most famous and most frequently visited of the Bronze-Age pounds. It covers an area of about 4 acres and the impressive outer wall is over 500yds in circumference. This was originally a double wall with a gap between the two, probably filled with rubble and earth. It has been estimated that when it was first built it was at least 6ft high.

Inside the pound there are the remains of animal pens and 24 huts, some with excellent angled protective entrances to keep the wind and the rain out of the doorway. There is a massive gateway on the south side with its paving stones still in position. It would have been closed with great baulks of timber. Excavations by the Dartmoor Exploration Committee found cooking holes and kitchen refuse, pottery and artefacts as well as post holes which must have supported the thatched or turf roofs of the huts. In some of the huts there was evidence of sleeping platforms. Such finds make it easier to imagine what life must have been like for these Bronze-Age people.

The pound was probably on the edge of the forest that clothed the lower slopes of the moors and valleys up to a height of about 1000ft, which although

Excavations at Grimspound, May 1894. The effect of mining is clearly visible on the hillside beyond.

The Revd Sabine Baring-Gould stands in the newly restored entrance to Grimspound, 1894.

Left: *The entrance to Grimspound.*

Above: *One of the hut circles within Grimspound.*

was the haunt of bears and wolves, was nevertheless the source of fuel for the settlement. The inhabitants of Grimspound would have grazed their animals on the slopes of Hameldown and Hookney Tor on either side. At night they would have driven their sheep, goats and cattle into the pound for protection – not only against wild animals but other marauding tribes. Their water supply still flows from Grimslake on the north side of the wall.

Climb up the well-defined track running south up **Hookney Tor**. You will see that it has been paved with slabs of granite to prevent erosion. The views from the top are good – look west to Princetown and the old television mast on Hessary Tor and north across the moor to Cosdon Hill. With your map you should be able to identify a whole range of tors, villages and other features.

On the north side of the tor look for one of the several paths that drop gently down to the road in a north-westerly direction. Cross over and look for a track that will lead you down to **Headland Warren Farm**. This is a remote and lonely place dating from the thirteenth century. I am always intrigued by the monkey puzzle trees growing beside the thatched buildings. A pub (known at

Headland Warren Farm.

*The north end of the stone row
at Headland Warren, 1894.*

one time as the Birch Tor Inn) once stood on this site and was frequented by the thirsty miners from the Headland Mine and the Birch Tor, Golden Dagger and Vitifer Mines. A sign used to hang outside that read:

Jan Roberts lives here,
Sells cider and beer,
Your hearts for to cheer,
And if you want meat,
To make up a treat,
Here be rabbits to eat.

What more would you want?!

Another owner of Headland Warren was a James Hannaford who, returning one dark night from the Warren House Inn to his home, fell down one of the many mine shafts in the area. Nobody has said how much beer or cider he had consumed but somehow, luckily, his fall was stopped by a wooden platform quite a long way down. It was too far to climb out and in spite of his shouts for help nobody heard him. However, his faithful collie remained by the shaft all night, whimpering and whining. Daylight came and search parties set out to look for James, the word having got round that he had not returned home. After a considerable time, attracted and guided by the collie's barks, they arrived at the shaft and were able to haul the old man out. As you would expect James Hannaford never forgot that he owed his life to his faithful dog. Eventually when he died James was buried in Widecombe-in-the-Moor, his coffin having been carried along the great ridge of Hamel Down on the Widecombe Way to the churchyard.

There is an obvious track that climbs up the hill, more or less west, once you have crossed over the stream.

If you are interested in having a look at the **triple stone row** marked on the map at the end of Challacombe Down then you must keep to the left towards the top and enter the maze of gullies or gerts here. With luck you should find the track that leads left to this fine stone row. There are larger stones at the north end of the row that is 170yds long, which probably led to a grave but a lot has been obscured and destroyed by the

The triple stone row on Challacombe Down.

miners digging their gerts. It is one of the highest triple rows on Dartmoor at a height of 1400ft.

Find your way back to the main track, probably with difficulty. Before you do so, you may like to explore these amazingly deep gashes hacked and blasted out of the hillside by the miners. The largest one is about 50ft deep. This is Chaw Gully. Chaw is a corruption of chough, the rare Cornish bird that once again is breeding on the Lizard. This bird is traditionally associated with King Arthur who, legend has it, was transformed on his death, into a chough.

Follow the track down and you will soon come to the valley floor and a delightful grassy area with quite a number of ruins around. A small stream, the Redwater Brook that joins the West Webburn River, flows under a stone bridge. The brook probably got its name because of the minerals in the water.

You are now standing in the heart of what was one of the busiest and most productive tin-mining areas of Dartmoor. By 1738 a certain Mr William Hatchcett visiting 'Vytifor Mine' found that over 13 shafts had already been dug by the earlier miners, one to a depth of 40 fathoms (mine depths are always given in fathoms).

In 1820 a Mr Paul, who was the owner of the **Vitifer Mine** at that time, found an even older, walled shaft of some 15 fathoms. There is evidence in the Earl of Devon's estate papers that members of the Gidley Family, yeomen of Throwleigh, were summoned to attend the stannary court in Chagford on 26 September 1750 in order to settle various disputes about ownership and payment of dues to Lord Courtenay concerning Vitifer Mine.

The Widecombe-in-the-Moor birth register reveals that in 1842 a Robert Merrit, named as a parent, was living at **Birch Tor Mine** and must have been 'captain of the mines'.

These early documents and many others besides reveal that there was a thriving mining industry and community at Birch Tor and Vitifer from early times. By the 1870s the underground workings had reached 70 fathoms and this was made possible by the invention of gunpowder used for blasting the shafts and gerts that previously had been laboriously hacked out by hand.

Stone bridge over Redwater Brook at Vitifer Mine.

Robert Burnard's famed photograph of Chaw Gully, near Vitifer Mine, May 1894. The figure is the Revd Baring-Gould.

Approximately 100 men worked in the mines in this area at this time. They walked to work from their homes in the surrounding villages on a Monday morning and stayed on for the rest of the week in lodgings at Postbridge or in the barracks at the mines themselves. There was also a counting-house on site.

A number of cottages were built by the miners on the slopes of Watern Hill near the Warren House Inn. They were known as West Cottages as they were west of the mines. However, they were very exposed to the elements and became known as Cape Horn! It was about this time that Newhouse Inn was rebuilt on the north side of the road; it eventually became the Warren House Inn of today.

Birch Tor and Vitifer Mines were worked separately even though they were adjacent to each other in the valley where you are standing. However, in 1845 the mines combined and in 1859 a new company, the New Birch Tor and Vitifer Consols, was created. It was a time of comparative prosperity with an average of 112 tons of black tin being mined each year in the mid-1860s. The record year was 1864 when 187.3 tons were recorded.

By the 1870s production was down drastically and mining stopped in 1883. From 1903 to 1915 work started again underground with some 35 men employed; 20 worked in the shafts and adits while the others were on the surface. The best production year was 1907 when 22.6 tons of ore were sold. All underground work stopped in 1915 but surface mining continued until 1926.

Between 1852, when records started, and 1913, 1300 tons of dressed ore were produced from the two mines; it is thus the most important tin-producing area on Dartmoor. Sadly not a lot remains and it is extraordinary to think that mining was going on here until the period between the two world wars.

As you stand on the bridge looking west, the first ruins on the left (just an outline of a low wall) are all that remain of the 'miners' dry'. A dry was a building where the miners, as they ended their shifts, would try to get warm again, change their clothes and attempt to dry the ones they were wearing, having worked all day soaked to the skin. The building must have been a great comfort for the men after they had walked up, not only from Birch Tor and Vitifer Mines but also Golden Dagger Mine, on windy, wet and cold winter days.

Until the 1950s, just beyond the dry, there stood a tall chimney which was probably an engine house to produce steam power. However both mines, particularly Birch Tor Mine, relied on water-wheels for power and it is possible to find the line of the leat that ran for 7 miles bringing water for the wheels.

Walk north up the valley towards one of the gerts and just before the track steepens have a look to your left and you will see one of the wheel pits now full of water and overgrown with heather, ferns and moss. Be sure to take care as it is rather treacherous under foot.

As you walk up to look at the wheel you will pass a number of ruins on your right, including a barracks where the miners lived, a smelting house, a smithy, dressing floors and a tramway to transport the ore from the various tunnels and adits known as 'levels'.

All that is left of the miners' dry at Vitifer Mine.

If you have time you might like to walk up to the Warren House Inn to get some refreshment. There is an obvious track that runs up from beyond the ruins of the dry towards the west. You probably won't want to stay the night!

Walk south from Birch Tor and Vitifer Mines towards Soussons Forest and go through the gate. As the whole area has been planted with conifers it is diffi-cult to visualise exactly how the mine was set out. This is **Golden Dagger Mine**. The hill that rises to the west is Dagger Hill. A possible explanation of the origins of the names is that a Bronze-Age dagger was found here and perhaps the bronze was mistaken for gold.

Follow the track for a short distance and look to your right; you will see some ruins of another miners' dry, with the remains of a large fireplace.

The stamps which crushed the mined ore at Golden Dagger Mine were driven by this huge water-wheel.

Walk a short distance north, past the dry, and follow the track into the old quarry. The main adit was driven in at the bottom of the slope but the entrance has been blocked with quarrying. As you enter the wider part of the quarry you will see, to your left, a small blocked gully with water pouring out from under the lower rocks. This must have been the main adit and the flow of water gives us an idea how wet these mines were. Along here once stood the main mine buildings, stamping mills and smith's shop, but all were knocked down.

The remains of the miners' dry at Golden Dagger Mine.

Dagger or Stamps wheel pit.

A deep gully, or openwork, leads out to your left in the quarry after the adit and with a struggle you can follow it for a while if you wish. However, it is easier to climb out of the quarry area near a loose pile of stones and rocks and turn left by the fence at the top and reach the deep gully further along.

I should warn you that the next section, if you are going to follow the deep openwork, makes for difficult walking; it is steep, with thick heather and wortleberry plants and many fallen and rotting tree trunks. There are many open shafts or gunnises about 14 fathoms deep until you come to the main machine shaft, which is 45 fathoms deep. All these shafts are fenced in with danger signs so you cannot get too close. The machine shaft was powered by a water-wheel on the north side and was used for pumping and drawing the ore.

Not much is known about the early history of Golden Dagger Mine although records show it was worked in 1860 and abandoned in 1866. It was opened again in 1880 by a man called Moses Bawden and produced tin almost continuously until 1913. It was owned by Dartmoor Minerals Ltd in 1905 but was taken over by Golden Dagger Mine Ltd under a Mr Thomas Settle. In 1892 23 men were working underground with another 18 on the surface; they produced 25.6 tons of black tin in that year but between 1880 and 1913 it mined some 220 tons of tin. During the Second World War, in 1940–42, the mine was prospected again in the hope of finding the value of the waste materials and alluvials.

If you go up the openwork to look at the shafts there is nothing to do other than to struggle back down again or to try to find a way down on the other side of the gulch. Either way, you need to get back down to ruins of the dry and find the track.

Keep to the left-hand route (do not set off right along the wide path through Soussons Forest). Cross over the Redwater Brook and walk south. After a short distance look to your right and you will see what looks like a low wall. A fairly indistinct path runs down to a little granite bridge over the stream. This leads you to the wall, which turns out to be the lower end of a wheel pit. This is Dagger or Stamps wheel pit of 1916, which housed a much broader wheel than was usual in the mines hereabouts. It is possible to see some of the huge timbers that secured the wheel bearing. It was used to drive Cornish drop hammers for crushing the ore. Just above the pit you can make out the leat running away north to collect water that ran down the valley from Vitifer Mine.

Return to the track and walk south. Just before the next ruin there is a sluice to the right of the track. Ahead are the ruins of what was known as Dinah's House. I have been unable to discover the identity of Dinah, but this building was home to some miners. On the right you can see the ground floor with its two entrances. This was the storeroom with a kitchen above. The bedrooms were on an upper floor, now gone of course, while on the left was an office and a lounge. Incredibly, it was inhabited until the 1940s, which may account for there being a garage on the extreme right end of the ruin, although I cannot imagine how anybody got a car down here!

Dinah's House.

Continue walking south down the track and after about 100yds, you will reach the ruins of an engine house on your left. Rather surprisingly, as major production finished in 1913, it was built in the 1920s. It used three different methods of obtaining power: water, gas and diesel. You can still see the foundations for the storage tank, a vapouriser, a fly-wheel pit and turbines and so on.

A little further on, to your right, you will see the remains of a buddle. There are quite a few of these on Dartmoor near the tin mines. Crushed tin ore in water was fed in over the central concrete core or boss. The heavier particles of tin settled in the centre near the core while the lighter debris floated to the outer rim. There were several long arms with brushes attached that rotated to prevent channels from forming and to mix the ore. This was a modern mechanical way of panning and streaming for ores.

Walk to the gate on the left. The signs tell you that the next part of the walk leads you round the south end of Challacombe Down. The valley is awash with bluebells in May and June. This is a delightful stretch as you cross open fields with wonderful views off to your right towards Soussons Farm and beyond, and the steep slopes of Challacombe Down above you to your left.

Above: *The buddle at Golden Dagger Mine.*

Above right: *A carpet of bluebells below Challacombe Down.*

This is one of the most extraordinary and fascinating areas of Dartmoor with a wealth of archaeological interest. Together the Dartmoor National Park Authority and English Heritage have produced large-scale maps of the ancient field systems and ruins from prehistoric to medieval times.

Soon the path swings round to the north and goes through a gate and a deep track down to Challacombe Farm and the medieval village. As you approach the farm look down to your right and you will see a fine example of a tinners' mould stone (there was a blowing house further on, by the West Webburn River, which later became a smithy for the community that settled in this valley). The mould stone was moved here by Mr Gordon Hambley, who farmed at Challacombe, so that visitors could see it.

There is little doubt that Bronze-Age people lived in this area but not much remains of their settlements as later buildings were constructed on the foundations and probably using the stones from the older huts. Certainly in medieval times this was a small and busy village. The manor of Challacombe is found in the Domesday Book of 1086. Documents dating back to 1244 and 1303 also made mention of Challacombe. In 1505 the Forester's accounts for the East Bailiwick make references to Cherlecombe or Chalnecombe. It said 'villat de Chalnecombe in parochia de Manaton vjd', in other words 'ville of Chalnecombe in the parish of Manaton 6d.' This refers to the venville, which is a term that comes from *fines villarum* meaning the rents of the vills, farms or small hamlets on the edge of Dartmoor. It is not clear when this system of rents and rights started, but they were linked to grazing, the gathering of stone and the cutting of peat; in return the people paid a small fee. In the case of Challacombe it was 6d. (2½p in modern money).

The vill of Challacombe had about 12 houses at one time that were grouped in this area. It has been suggested that 'Challow Combe' means 'combe of the calves' and that the calves were probably red deer. The people who lived in the venville lands were considered to be the special tenants of the king and had duties to perform, such as helping at the drifts or collecting animals (mainly ponies) off the moor. For this work they could demand a halfpenny cake! In the time of Henry VIII a document was drawn up: 'Instructions for my Lord Prince to the King's most honourable Council concerning my Lord Prince's Forest of Dartmoor'. It stated that the people of the venvilles could have more or less what they wanted except green oak and venison!

As you walk down the track it leads past the modern farmhouse built around the turn of the last century. The upper floor of the old barn behind the house was used as a chapel, a school and a meeting place until the new farm was built.

Just beyond the farmhouse and to the left, go through the gate to see remains of the *early-medieval village*. In 1613 there were five tenements recorded at **Challacombe** known as North Challacombe, North Middle Challacombe, South Middle Challacombe, South Challacombe, and East Challacombe. These were still named thus until the eighteenth century. The remains of all these tenements are more or less visible today except East Challacombe, which now lies under modern farm buildings.

The tinners' mould stone discovered at Challacombe Farm.

The medieval village at Challacombe.

Some of the buildings here, as well as the medieval buildings, were traditional Dartmoor longhouses, that were inhabited until the late-eighteenth century and possibly later. Indeed one of the buildings became a cider-house used by the thirsty miners in the nineteenth century. It is probable that the farmers at Challacombe were also miners and would walk to the Golden Dagger Mine or East Vitifer to work.

Quite clearly there was a fluctuating population at Challacombe and it has been suggested that, like the Hound Tor village, the plague in 1348 caused people to desert the area. The Earl of Devon had lands here and in 1797 the venville rights were drawn up for Challacombe; people were allowed to keep six-score sheep, 12 bullocks and one horse or 14 bullocks and no horse. It also stated that 'five Tenements in the Small Village called Challacombe and One Water Mill. This Part is very poor Cold and Hungry Ground, full of Rocks and Naturally healthy' – whatever that means!

Go north through the gate past Challacombe Cottages, which replaced some earlier buildings. These are still inhabited. Another gate will lead you out into grassy meadows with a marvellous feeling of space and open skies with Hookney Tor on the far horizon. After 50yds or so look down to your right for a sycamore tree growing by the small stream of the West Webburn and on the far side of the stream you will see a low wall which was the site of the mill mentioned in 1303. Also when the Earl of Devon had a survey made of his estates in 1774 a grist water-mill at Challacombe was mentioned.

The remains of the water-mill at Challacombe.

As you walk north along a ruined wall you will be below the remains of the farming at Challacombe, the largest surviving group of medieval strip lynchets in Dartmoor National Park. A lynchet is a bank formed by contour ploughing along a slope with an artificial barrier such as a low stone wall or unploughed soil on the lower edge – in other words terraces were created so that the steep land could be cultivated or left to grass. To strengthen the bank it was ploughed tight to the wall. The farmers of Challacombe ploughed their lynchets over a long period, so they gradually became larger and larger. They staggered the ends of the strips so that they could move their ox ploughs from one terrace to another. The best way to see these lynchets is from the road that you may have driven up on the other side of the valley to

The lynchets on Challacombe Down.

reach the start of this walk. They also benefit from being seen in low evening or winter sunlight.

Keep walking north along a springy, grassy track. After about a quarter of a mile there is a wheel pit below you to your right. This was for a large nine-teenth-century water-wheel which powered the pumping rods for the East Birch Tor Mine. It is worth walking down to have a look but take care as the pit is deep and full of water.

Back on the walk, you can probably make out the remains of the leat that brought the water to the wheel. When you get near the boundary of Headland Warren Farm you might just be able to make out the gullies that were dug to hold the pumping rods. Water from the leat turned the wheel, which was attached to the rods that slid backwards and forwards on each rotation. These rods stretched over half a mile to the shafts near Headland Warren Farm to work the pumps. What a sight it must have been.

All that is left now is for you to walk up to Headland Warren Farm on the right of way. Sadly it is no longer the Birch Tor Inn and Jan Roberts is no longer here to offer you cider and beer and rabbit pie! Depending where you left your car, work your way back up to the road to end what, I think, is one of the most fascinating walks into history on Dartmoor.

WALK 3

Castle Drogo, Hunter's Path to Hunter's Tor, Fisherman's Path, Fingle Bridge, Cranbrook Castle, The Angler's Rest, The Hunter's Path.

START: Car park at Castle Drogo. Map ref. (of castle): 722902.
Medium. 5.5. miles/9km. Moderate.

There is a café just beside the National Trust car park. Back down the road, which you probably came along to reach Castle Drogo, is the Sandy Park Inn and you will be walking to The Angler's Rest. In Drewsteignton there is another excellent pub, the Drewe Arms, so there are no shortages of places to get refreshments and sustenance for this walk!

You may wish to begin this walk in different places other than the car park at Castle Drogo. For example, you could start at the Angler's Rest at Fingle Bridge (map ref.: 743899). Dogmarsh Bridge (map ref.: 713894) is another starting place but parking is difficult here unless you are staying at the hotel by the bridge.

You will have to decide if you want to look round Castle Drogo before or after the walk. It is worth a visit and you will need to allow enough time to see both the castle and gardens. A guide book and entrance tickets can be bought at the desk by the café. The walk could well take you three or four hours or more, if you climb up to Cranbrook Castle, and longer if you stop at the Angler's Rest!

Castle Drogo was the last castle to be built in Britain; it took twenty years to complete, starting in 1911. A castle with twentieth-century comfort and amenities, it was the vision of two remarkable men: Julius Drewe and Edwin Lutyens. The former was born in 1856 and came from a long line of respectable professional families who had an interest in their ancestry. His father was the Revd George Smith Drew, vicar of Pulloxhill near Ampthill in Bedfordshire, who became a lecturer in theology at Cambridge in his later life.

Castle Drogo.

Julius' grandfather had been a tea broker in London while the family of his wife, Mary Peek, were also involved in the tea trade. Not surprisingly then, by the age of 21 Julius was buying tea in the Far East for the firm of Peek Bros & Winch in Liverpool. After enjoying these exciting travels as a young man, he founded his first shop in Liverpool, The Willow Pattern Tea Shop, in 1878.

This small shop thrived and with typical Victorian enterprise the two took a loan of £10 000 (a considerable sum for those days) and in 1883 opened a shop in London known by the marvellously patriotic name of The Home and Colonial Stores. It was at this time that such stores as Sainsbury's and Lipton's were opening, satisfying a demand by urban working classes for basic foods at competitive prices. Drew and and his partner, John Musker, had hit the market at exactly the right time. They opened stores in Birmingham and Leeds and in many of the larger towns in England. They also started a chain of smaller shops known as 'tea stores'. By 1890 there were over 100 stores across the country.

Initially, Drew was directly involved – he was responsible for much of the buying and with his knowledge of the tea trade he favoured Indian tea, which soon overtook Chinese tea in popularity in Britain. He also introduced margarine into his stores, which alongside butter was very popular.

After only six years, when Julius was just thirty-three, the business had done so well that both Drew and Musker were wealthy men and they were able to step back from the everyday running of the stores. He handed over the running of the company to a William Slaughter who was a relative by marriage and who became chairman of the company for thirty years. Slaughter was a solicitor, obviously with an eye for business; by 1906 there were over 500 branches in the country. With a 15 per cent dividend paid each year, Julius Drew, who held the majority of shares, became extremely rich.

By 1890 he had married Frances Richardson and they were able to buy a mock castle called Culverden near Tunbridge Wells. The couple lived there for nine years during which time they had three sons. The first, Adrian, born in 1891 was sadly killed in Flanders in 1917. The second boy, Basil, who was born in 1894 became a barrister while the third, Cedric, born in 1896 became an MP. Two daughters, Mary and Frances, were born in 1900 and 1907.

The family moved, in 1899, to a mansion, Wadhurst Hall. It was built of red brick in 1870 for two Spanish bachelor brothers, both merchants who traded in South America. Drew was able to buy the mansion following a set of unfortunate circumstances. Living with the brothers at Wadhurst Hall was a third brother José who, with his beautiful and clever Spanish wife, used to entertain the aristocracy in a lavish and extravagant style. The Prince of Wales was often to be seen at the house and on shooting parties. However, it all ended in disaster as a result of non-payment of bonds by the Argentinians in 1890 which made all the brothers bankrupt. This caused monetary tremors within the financial house of Baring (a name that cropped up in 1995 with another financial crisis).

Drew took advantage of this as the brothers were forced to sell not only the mansion but all the glorious Spanish furniture and tapestries they had collected. Drew moved in and bought the lot. Many of these exotic furnishings are now to be seen in Castle Drogo, but we are jumping ahead with the story.

Julius Drew wished to be known as somebody more than the owner of a chain of grocery stores and the 'margarine king' as he has been called rather unkindly. Buying Wadhurst Hall certainly helped towards that and he became a JP in

The rear of Castle Drogo.

1900. He even reached the dizzy heights of being included in Burke's *Landed Gentry*, listed as 'Drew of Wadhurst Hall'.

Both Julius and his two brothers were interested in their ancestry and after some research they traced the family history back to their great-grandfather Thomas Drew, a London surveyor who had links with lands in Devon. Their mother's family, whose maiden name was Peek, also came from Devon. The research led them to Broadhembury near Honiton, where a family called Drewe had once owned property, which happened to be for sale. Keen to pursue his Devon roots Julius bought the small estate in 1901 and renovated a farmhouse that became Broadhembury House, where his brother William went to live. It was at this time that Julius changed his name to Drewe with the 'e'.

The plot, which leads to Castle Drogo, thickens. The genealogist discovered that there was a possible family link with a Norman baron called Dru, which translates to Drogo in its Latin form, who came over to England with William the Conqueror. Another descendant called Drogo de Teigne gave his name to the village of Drewsteignton in the twelfth century, which is near Castle Drogo.

The quite extraordinary end to the story comes with the fact that Richard Peek, who was Julius' first cousin, was the vicar of Drewsteignton and Julius visited him on many occasions. From those visits must have come the vision to build a castle near where his ancient ancestors must have lived, worked and walked. He was faced with the question: who to design and build it? Julius had the money so it had to be the best; an imposing castle, set as it was to be above the gorge of the River Teign, near the vale of Chagford. This is where the second remarkable man comes on the scene: Edwin Landseer Lutyens.

Julius had probably heard of Lutyens because of the many country houses he had designed and built in Surrey, Sussex and Kent, some of which were quite close to Wadhurst Hall. The gardens of these houses were designed by Lutyens and his friend Gertrude Jekyll.

Lutyens, perhaps the greatest architect of the twentieth century, was born in London in 1869 and studied at the RCA. By 1889 he had his own practice. He felt a close affinity with the vernacular style and used traditional building methods and materials for his country houses. However, he began to move towards a monumental classical style with such projects as Tigbourne Court in

Surrey and Lindisfarne Castle in Northumberland. Incidentally, I came across this classical grandeur when I visited the city of New Delhi with its government buildings and Vice-Regal Palace, now Presidential Palace, all designed by Lutyens in 1912–31. He also designed the British Embassy in Washington DC and many other prestigious buildings, as well as over fifty First World War memorials including the Whitehall Cenotaph. He was the perfect choice for Julius; the man to design and build a spectacular ancestral home.

Lutyens, however, was a busy man completing his work of the Hampstead Garden Suburb, drawing up designs for a memorial to Edward VII in Trafalgar Square, the British Pavilion for the Rome Exhibition and the Rand Regiment Memorial in South Africa. It was this work in the British dominions that led to his commission in India for the Viceroy's House I mentioned earlier. It is said that Lutyens worked on sketches and plans for Castle Drogo while travelling to India by P&O – he had a cabin set out as a drawing office.

It appears that by August 1910 Lutyens had been commissioned to design and build Castle Drogo, although he had doubts about the size of the project. He wrote in a letter, 'Only I do wish he didn't want a castle but just a delicious, loveable house with plenty of large good rooms in it!' However, before Julius could realise his dreams of building a castle that befits a man descended from a Norman baron he had to get hold of some land, preferably near Drewsteignton, where he believed his ancestral estates lay. The old adage, 'it's not what you know, but who you know' is rather fitting here. You will remember that his cousin was the vicar of Drewsteignton and it so happened that the land where Drogo Castle now stands was glebe land. I wonder what the bishop thought about the selling of church land? Julius bought the land in 1910 and over the years acquired more and more ground around the site including the other side of the gorge called Whiddon Park. Eventually the estate was 1500 acres.

The early sketches included a huge building that incorporated a keep, towers and courtyards, which conveyed a feeling of it being a castle to be defended against all comers. Such a grand concept proved impractical and a much more manageable set of sketches and plans were drawn up reducing the size of the castle by two-thirds. However the vast and impressive granite wing from these early sketches survived; it took twenty years to build.

On Drewe's fifty-fifth birthday, 4 April 1911, the foundation stone of Castle Drogo was laid. Granite from Merrivale on Dartmoor, Blackinstone and Pew

Castle Drogo's main tower.

Tor was quarried and brought to the site. All went well for the first year with the castle being built, on Drewe's insistence, by traditional methods. The snag was that Lutyens had forgotten to get planning permission! It is not clear how he got round that but one can imagine the problem these days if one started to build a castle within the Dartmoor National Park without planning permission! It was not until 1913 that the final plans were settled for the rest of the building. The First World War intervened and slowed up the construction.

During the building Drewe rented a house in Torquay which he later bought. He and Lutyens would visit the site together, to check on progress at Drogo.

By 1924 Castle Drogo was finished just enough for Julius and his family to be able to stay there on occasions. On 22 December 1925 the last stone was put in place on the main castle and the cranes and scaffolds were taken away. The Drewe family was able to move to its ancestral home; a dream come true. The gardens were also being laid out and it is probable that Gertrude Jekyll had a hand in the design and certainly ideas from India were used by Lutyens who had seen gardens there while working in New Delhi.

The gardens at Castle Drogo.

There is a sad ending to this story as Julius suffered a stroke in 1924 and died in Torquay in 1931 having lived only a few years at Castle Drogo. He was buried in Drewsteignton churchyard and his granite tombstone was designed, appropriately, by Sir Edwin Lutyens who lived until 1944. He was knighted in 1918 and was able to see the finished grandeur of the last castle to be built in Britain: a vision of two men.

Julius' second son Basil lived at the castle until his death in 1974. That year Basil's son Anthony and grandson Dr Christopher Drewe gave Castle Drogo to the National Trust.

Starting at the Castle Drogo car park, walk back down the drive by which you arrived and after about 40yds on your right there is an almost-hidden path that leads you to the **Hunter's Path**.

At a junction which you reach quickly signs will tell you that you can follow the Hunter's Path left to Fingle Bridge or right down to the **Fisherman's Path**. I suggest that you go right and follow the broad path high above the Teign Gorge with marvellous views down to the river. Soon the track steepens and then flattens again by a line of beeches just before you arrive at a road that leads to Coombe Farm. Turn left and follow this. There are signs all the way. Don't follow the drive to the farm but fork left on the path past a thatched house and descend to the river by **Hunter's Tor**.

On the opposite bank of the River Teign there is the ancient Whiddon deer park which is one of the estates that Julius Drewe bought to add to the lands around Castle Drogo. The medieval deer park (still home to fallow deer) is surrounded by an 8ft-high granite wall built by Sir John Whiddon in the sixteenth century. It is a Site of Special Scientific Interest and a wildlife sanctuary, with ancient trees, mainly oak and ash, and an amazing range of lichens and wildlife.

The path takes you east along the river with the constant sound of the moorland water in your ears tumbling down over the rocks and through deep pools. It is worth noting that in times of heavy storms the Teign will be a raging torrent roaring like thunder down the gorge. After a while you come to Drewe's Weir where, if you are lucky, you might see salmon using the fish ladder beside the weir to get upstream to spawn.

The tomb of Julius Drewe in Drewsteignton churchyard.

Teign Gorge.

Above: *Hunter's Tor.*

Above right: *The weir in flood.*

The tranquil River Teign.

The next point of interest is to your right. The logan-stone, a little downstream from the weir, is a huge block of granite balancing on another. It stands beside the river down a steep drop and once rocked backwards and forwards with a gentle push but sadly no longer. It was also called the 'moving rock' by the Revd John Swete, that great West-Country traveller who wrote about it in his diary in 1792. He claimed it was 10ft high and 18ft long, which is not quite true. He must have been a little overexcited by the atmosphere near the river!

Probably in those days otters lived and bred in the Teign in great numbers but even though their numbers are increasing today, after a huge decline, they are shy, illusive creatures and you would be very fortunate to see one. The little black-and-white bird you will certainly see is the dipper, as it darts along the river from boulder to boulder, just above the water and then dives below the surface seeming almost to fly underwater. You may even see a flash of electric blue – a kingfisher in flight or sometimes sitting on a favourite branch beside the water with a small fish hanging out of its beak.

On the opposite side of the river in Whiddon Wood is the turbine house which was built in 1927. Hydro-electric power was used at Castle Drogo; turbines

produced electricity from the waters of the Teign. There were two turbines one of which was still working up until 1994. This smaller one was for use in the summer when the demand was less, while a larger turbine, undergoing repairs at the time of writing, was used during the winter. The National Trust hopes to restore both turbines in order to produce electricity for the castle.

Above left: *The turbine house in Whiddon Wood.*

Above: *The logan-stone or 'moving rock'.*

Mainly oak grows in Whiddon Wood and at one stage the bark was collected after felling to be used for curing leather because of its high tannin content. Coppicing (cutting the main trunk of a tree almost to ground level so that many stems then shoot from the bole) took place here as part of the forestry husbandry. Hazel, oak, sweet chestnut and ash can all be used in this way so that rotation cropping can take place. The small timber produced from this system was used for charcoal burning and the platforms where the burning mounds were made for slow combustion, can be seen all over the wood.

Further on, to your left, are the rocks of Sharp Tor. Unlike the granite found elsewhere on Dartmoor, this tor is formed from the carboniferous, sedimentary rocks of the Culm Measures which stretch across north Devon and Cornwall to the coast, where they appear as cliffs with extraordinary folds of strata, such as at Bude. The Culm Measures here are especially interesting as they were baked and changed by the heat of the molten granite welling up to produce what is known as the metamorphic aureole; a circle of metamorphosed rocks in a ring around the edge of Dartmoor. Beside the ridge of rocks of Sharp Tor there is a scree slope – a steep slope of loose rocks that have broken off from the main rock-face as a result of erosion. I remember, a great many years ago, when I was looking for climbing routes here, that a kestrel was nesting on one of the ledges.

Move along the Fisherman's Path, past another weir, until you arrive at **Fingle Bridge**. This is a delightful spot but it can be crowded at peak holiday times. This bridge dates back to Elizabethan times. It was on an important packhorse route between Moretonhampstead and Drewsteignton; it was a vital crossing point as the next bridge was either a long way downriver at Steps Bridge or upriver at Dogmarsh Bridge. The packhorses carried flour from Fingle Mill as well as the charcoal and the bark for tanning from Whiddon Wood.

Fingle Bridge.

Fingle Bridge, from a nineteenth-century print.

The mill was a little downstream and you can wander along the old mill leat for about 200yds in order to reach its ruins. It was destroyed in 1894 by a fire that the miller and his wife tried to put out with buckets of water. They managed to get their children out of the building before it collapsed.

Now another decision! If you fancy a strenuous and long climb of nearly 1000ft and about three-quarters of a mile, then cross the river and start up what was once the old packhorse road (now really only a track) from Fingle Bridge to Moretonhampstead. It winds up through Charles Wood. Keep an eye open for a granite cross. This is the Cavaliers Cross and is said to be where a Royalist was killed in a Roundhead ambush. There are other tales of the Civil War in the area. A field nearby called Blood Park is where a battle was fought in which Sidney Godolphin was fatally wounded in 1642. He was a Cavalier poet and after he was wounded he was taken, as a prisoner, by the Royalists to the family home of the Whyddons in Chagford where he died. The old house near the church is now the Three Crowns Hotel and if you look in the alcove over the door you will see the bust of Sidney Godolphin.

The ruins of the old mill downstream from Fingle Bridge.

Back to the climb! If you made it, you will arrive, via some fields, at a track to the right that will lead you to **Cranbrook Castle**. This is an Iron-Age fort, of which there are three within a few miles of each other above the River Teign: Cranbrook, where you are now, Prestonbury Castle just across the valley on the other side of the river which you can see and, downstream, just over a mile away, is Wooston Castle. They were all built in magnificent, commanding situations guarding the gorge of the River Teign. In some ways these forts are the largest and most dramatic features remaining of the prehistoric world. There are over 70 of them in Devon and, while they have been investigated, archaeologists are still not clear as to their use. It is unclear whether they were occupied all the time or whether the people withdrew into them during times of inter-tribal fighting. It has been suggested that newcomers built the forts around the edges of Dartmoor (there are none on the moor itself) to defend themselves from the more established Bronze-Age people living on the high moor.

The ramparts of Cranbrook Castle.

The Revd John Swete, who wrote about the 'moving rock' in his diary, visited the site of Cranbrook in 1789. In 1901 the castle was excavated. Slingstones and bits of wood were found in one of the inner ditches while near one of the entrances and against the ramparts the remains of two houses in which charcoal, pottery and a rotary quern for grinding corn were found.

Looking towards Fingle Bridge down the Teign Gorge, 1889.

It is quite a difficult area to appreciate as the whole site is covered with gorse and bracken. However, the area of the fort is about 6–7 acres and there is a circular, central encampment as well as a smaller one which was never completed, all with a surrounding rampart of stone and turf. To the south the inner slope of the rampart is about 20ft, while the outer slope is about 40ft, beyond which there are the remains of two ditches. As has occurred on many archaeological sites, a large quantity of the stones and rocks from the ramparts was robbed by farmers and those making the roads. The entrances would have been the most vulnerable areas and it has been suggested that these would have had heavy, wooden gates in place across them, while along the top of the ramparts there might have been a palisade of timbers set close together. However, few hard facts have emerged about these impressive forts.

If you walked up to Cranbrook Castle then I am afraid that there is nothing for it but a knee-bashing descent back to Fingle Bridge and probably a welcome stop at the *Angler's Rest*!

The Angler's Rest.

Walk north for 100yds or so past the pub, keeping an eye out for the sign on your left directing you to the **Hunter's Path**. This marvellous path climbs quite steeply to the Hunting Gate and then contours high above the gorge of the Teign and eventually Sharp Tor. This is very different vegetation and habitat to the woods and forests of the lower path. It is open heathland, although it was once woodland; the trees were felled to create more rough grazing. The whole of this region, Piddledown Common, was once an area of heathland but by enclosing some stretches on the top and ploughing and planting grass seed a lot of the heathland has been lost and pasture fields created. This is a marvellous environment for an amazing number of butterflies including the rare high brown fritillary. Bird life includes stonechats and tree and meadow pipits. As a result of the decrease in the amount of grazing, trees are beginning to return to the heathland and today there are small stands of silver birch.

Fingle Mill, captured by photographer Robert Burnard, August 1892. Shortly after this the mill was destroyed in a fire.

There are several places along this path where you will get tremendous views of Dartmoor, the Teign Gorge and Castle Drogo. It is possible to get to Drogo from this path and if you bought your ticket before you started the walk you are now in a position to go in and look around. You should recognise the place where you joined the Hunter's Path at the start of the walk. Ahead of you is a sign that says No Entry. This is the entrance to Mr Drewe's Path. If you have your ticket you can follow this path, which runs parallel and just above the path you walked along at the beginning. It will lead you up through a dark tunnel of holly trees to the back of the the castle, near the restaurant. By cutting through the trimmed yews you will find yourself at the imposing front of Castle Drogo. Alternatively, you may wish to gather your strength by visiting the café and then returning to the castle later. Either way, I really recommend a visit.

The entrance gate, with its 644lb working portcullis with octagonal turrets and the heraldic Drewe lion carved by Herbert Palliser, leads you into the castle. It has a library and billiard-room, drawing-room, dining-room, a butler's sitting-room, a servant's drying-room, a pantry, a switch-room where the electricity from the turbines on the Teign was controlled, a kitchen, scullery and larder. The bedrooms and bathroom are upstairs. Most poignant is the bedroom of Adrian Drewe, killed at Ypres on 12 July 1917, which is a memorial to him. The castle also has a gun-room and chapel. In many rooms and corridors are splendid tapestries and oil paintings. There is a sense that the Drewes have just gone out for a short while and will

Above: *The portcullis above the main door of Castle Drogo.*

Right: *The lion and Drewe motto over the main door of the castle.*

be back any minute; it is an extraordinary glimpse into the world of nineteenth- and twentieth-century gentry.

Drogo Nomen et Virtus Arma Dedit proclaims the Drewe motto over the door, meaning 'Drewe is the name and valour gave it arms.' That says it all.

WALK 4

ROUND POUND, KES TOR, SHOVEL DOWN, TEIGN-E-VER CLAPPER BRIDGE,
SCORHILL CIRCLE, BATSWORTHY CORNER.

**START: There is room to park near the entrance to Batsworthy
House but please do not block the drive. Map ref.: 663865.
Medium. 3.75 miles/6 km. Easy.**

Chagford, a pleasant moorland village is 2 miles away with all the facilities
you might expect in a small community including an outstanding restaurant, 22 Mill Street. Also close by is another first-class hotel and restaurant,
Gidleigh Park, as well as many other excellent hotels and B&Bs.

As you drove to the parking place you will have passed, on
your right, just beside the road, a large stone circle, known
as **Round Pound**. It is worth walking back to have a closer
look before you walk up to Kes Tor. There are two concentric circles; the inner one was the wall of a large hut and the
other radiating walls formed pens or small courts. The site
was excavated by Lady Aileen Fox, in 1951–52, who was the
eminent archaeologist from Exeter responsible for work on
the medieval village at Hound Tor (Walk 1). She found evidence at Round Pound of early iron smelting, the only
instance on Dartmoor. It has been dated as Iron Age or
about 500BC. She discovered an iron-smelting furnace, a
forging pit and slag all in the central hut. The iron ore could
have been brought from the Hennock area (about 9 miles
away) where micaceous haematite was mined until the
1930s. Foale's Arrishes was the only other Iron-Age settlement on Dartmoor (also Walk 1) but no evidence of smelting
was found there.

Round Pound.

The main hut at Round Pound is very large for Dartmoor, being about 37ft across. The only entrance faces south-east and was cobbled with steps up, to prevent water flowing into the interior. It was flanked with horizontal granite slabs. The hut had been divided into two sections. The west side was where the people lived and carried out their iron working. Remains of pottery were found here and it appears that oak and hazel were burnt on the fire. Standing against the wall was a granite slab about 6in. wide that had been used to sharpen the various iron implements that had been made.

The other room was where the iron ore was smelted; it contained a clay-lined pit in which charcoal and slag were found. This was probably the furnace that would have been made by a domed lid of wet clay being constructed over the hole, forming what is known as a bowl furnace. To create the intense heat needed to melt the iron out of the ore bellows were used; near the furnace hole was another granite slab where it was thought the bellows would have stood.

Other amazing details of the iron-forging work were also discovered near the furnace, such as a pit where the iron was reheated to become white hot for forging and shaping. Near this was a depression, about 3ft in diameter, that would have been filled with water where the red-hot iron could be cooled down after hammering. A covered drain from this ran to the outside of the hut linking up with a drain from the living quarters.

About a dozen post holes were unearthed; it is believed they supported a roof thatched with reeds and heather. The central area of the roof was probably left open so that smoke and fumes could escape, and light could get in.

The work here by Lady Fox was one of the most important, landmark excavations ever carried out on Dartmoor. It must have been enormously exciting as more and more finds came to light and a clearer understanding of how these Iron-Age people lived and worked was revealed. All over Round Pound there is a highly developed system of prehistoric fields, drove roads and huts, for which plans were drawn up as early as 1857–58 by G.W. Ormerod of Chagford.

As you walk up towards **Kestor Rock**, in a south-south-easterly direction, you will pass along the edge of these fields and a square pound. Flints, arrowheads, knives and scrapers have all been found in this area. As there are no flints to be found on Dartmoor these early flint tools were probably made of

Kestor Rock.

chert, a type of flint found near Exeter on Haldon Hill and near Sidmouth; it must have been brought from there to the moor. I have a marvellous mental picture of these canny, early traders journeying up to barter the flints with the moorland farmers and iron workers in return for meat, skins or even iron implements.

Kestor Rock is clearly visible as you climb the hill towards it. In fact, this rock can be seen from miles around and the views from the top are excellent both over the moor and the surrounding countryside. Once on top you will discover one of the largest rock basins on a Dartmoor tor, as well as many smaller ones. The largest one is about 8ft across and 6ft 8in. wide when full of water. G.W. Ormerod, who made a plan of the prehistoric field systems nearby, discovered the basin to be full of peat and stones, in the 1850s, which he removed only to be told by local farmers that it had been filled in about a century before to prevent sheep from falling in! He then made arrangements for iron railings to be put round the basin, which remained in place for over one hundred years. You can see the holes that were drilled for the uprights. Dartmoor legends have it that these basins were made by Druids probably for sinister, sacrificial purposes. This isn't true of course; they are the result of erosion by water and frost.

Strike out south-west aiming at a tall standing stone about half a mile away. This menhir is known as the Longstone. It stands about 10.5ft high and carved on it are the letters 'C' for Chagford, 'G' for Gidleigh and 'DC' for the Duchy of Cornwall. It forms the boundary marker for the two parishes as well as the Forest of Dartmoor. Like so many of these ancient boundary stones it was mentioned in the perambulation of 1240. The purpose of this perambulation was to set the outer boundaries of the Forest of Dartmoor and mark the extent of the royal hunting lands according to a Charter of the Forest granted to King John in 1215 and later to Henry III in 1224. However the first recorded agreement to the bounds came in 1240 when the forest was granted to Richard, Earl of Cornwall. It was at this point that the Longstone was mentioned as one of the markers. Of course, the stone had not originally been erected for this purpose but had been erected on that spot during the Bronze Age; it was used by the people of medieval times and others as a convenient marker.

You are now on **Shovel Down** (which sometimes goes by the marvellous name of Shuggledown). All around you are remains of the Bronze-Age Beaker folk. The name Beaker came from the fact that clay urns and pots with distinctive

The Longstone, Shovel Down.

Stone rows on Shovel Down.

patterns on them were found in some of the graves. This is an extraordinary area for prehistoric remains. If you walk just over 200yds south from the Longstone you will come across a single block of granite that once formed the cover stone of a dolmen (burial chamber). It has the name Three Boys which I suspect means that at one time, there must have been three stones standing here; sadly no more – this is another example of stones being taken away from antiquities for building or repairing other buildings.

Go back to the Longstone and walk north. You will come across a line of stone rows, sometimes double, leading back to where the burial chamber of Three Boys once stood. Indeed many of the stone rows on Dartmoor lead to a cairn or kistvaen that was used for burial. You will pass another smaller standing stone as you walk on, as well as two cairns until you come to an unusual stone circle. The main ring is about 29ft across but it encloses three others. There are ten other multiple stone circles such as this on Dartmoor. The stones in the row leading to the circle gradually get bigger as they get nearer the circle and lying close to the ring are two fallen menhirs; one is over 7ft long and flat topped while the other is nearly 12ft tall and is slim. When standing they must have formed an impressive and majestic entrance to the circle. I wonder what ceremonies took place here? Perhaps they represent male and female?

There are two more standing stones on the edge of the hill. They were the remains of another dolmen. Even if you do not find these stones, walk north to the corner of the wall to your right and down to the North Teign River where you will find ***Teign-e-ver Bridge***. This is an odd name; it is probably a broad Dartmoor dialect corruption of Teign Ford, which becomes Teign-a-ford and on to Teign-e-ver. This is a lovely spot with the infant Teign in a deep gully before cascading over rocks into deep pools, while all around are mountain ash trees leaning over the brown, peaty water.

Further west the Walla Brook enters the Teign and the peninsula between the two streams is where tinners once worked. Indeed, like the East Dart at Sandy Hole there are sections where they walled up the banks of the rivers to increase the flow of water. There is another clapper bridge over the Walla Brook. As there are large slabs of granite in the river and a high granite wall on the right bank it is likely that there was an important bridge here in medieval times, which was 'swept away by a great flood in 1826' as Crossing writes.

A clapper bridge over the infant River Teign.

The tolmen in 1889.

The tolmen or Holed Stone beside the Teign, 2002.

Cross over this clapper bridge and walk back downstream to the Teign and continue for about 50yds past the confluence. In the bed of the river, amongst the mass of boulders, you will see the extraordinary tolmen or Holed Stone. The word 'tolmen' comes from the Celtic 'tol' meaning hole and 'maen' meaning stone. The hole is about a yard across and if you are fairly agile you can climb through it. Like the rock basins on Kestor Rock it was said to have been made and used by the Druids for sinister rituals. Similar to the Men An Tol (the same corruption of the Celtic words) on the Land's End peninsula in Cornwall this tolmen is said to have magic properties, which will bring good luck, make wishes come true and even cure whooping cough if you crawl through!

Below the tolmen the river goes in to a steep wooded gorge. Return to the bridge and walk up the hill to your right and you will find a well-made track which passes over the Gidleigh Leat by yet another clapper bridge. This will lead you to **Scorhill Circle**, probably one of the most impressive stone circles on Dartmoor. It lies in the wide basin of the North Teign and can be seen from miles around. The Revd Samuel Rowe writing in 1848 waxed lyrical about it

Scorhill stone circle, 1889.

by stating that 'the sacred circle of Scorhill is by far the finest example of the rude, but venerable shrines of Druidical worship in Devonshire'. Sadly, like many other remains on Dartmoor a great many of the stones have been stolen or knocked down, many before 1800.

Accounts of the numbers of stones in the circle vary enormously. Why not count them yourself and see what you come up with?

There were probably 65–70 stones originally and even though a cart track cuts unceremoniously through the circle it still is a mysterious and magical place. The tallest stone is just over 8ft high on the north-west side and on the south-south-west edge there is a massive slab over 6ft long and 5ft wide lying on the ground. It is unclear as to the exact use of these Bronze-Age circles but it may be that they formed a sort of meeting-place for worship or ceremony. If you stand in the centre of the circle you will see the most northerly moon set over the tip of the tallest stone. As it is set radially to the circumference of the circle it suggests that this supposition is a real possibility.

The stone circle at Scorhill.

It is also possible that taller stones were robbed. You will see that some of the stones lying outside the circle have been tampered with and there are another two that have had holes made in them for splitting. In this case a local farmer of recent times was looking for gateposts. He was stopped from removing them when he was caught in the act!

Make your way back to the clapper bridges over the leat, the Walla Brook and the Teign. Climb up the hill to the south-south-east wall and follow it back to **Batsworthy Corner**. Turn north and you will be back at your car.

WALK 5

OKEHAMPTON CASTLE.

START: Car park for the castle. Map ref.: 582943.
Medium. 4.5 miles/7.25km.

Turn up the road by the White Hart Hotel at the traffic lights in Okehampton. About 200yds along there are signs on your right that lead you to Okehampton Castle, which is under the guardianship of English Heritage. You will have to pay an entrance fee and there is an excellent book-let on sale to guide you around the site. The town of Okehampton has all the facilities that you might want.

While walking around the castle does not cover a great distance there is a very pleasant circular walk from the castle that takes you along the bottom of the valley of the West Okement River through water meadows. It will probably take you about 45 minutes.

Alternatively you can take a linear walk from the castle to Meldon Viaduct and the dam and back again. In this instance, look for the path by the car park that ducks down an overgrown alley to the footbridge over the West Okement (there are signs). See page 67 for more about this short walk.**

Okehampton Castle lies in a valley but was built on a spur that stands high above the West Okement River. There was a ford across the river here and roads ran along the valley into Cornwall and back into the borough of Okehampton, which was growing at the time the castle was built. There were three large manors in the district which were mentioned in the Domesday Book. This is also where we get the first reference to Okehampton Castle. There is documentary evidence that the castle lay within the estates of a

Okehampton Castle, from a nineteenth-century print.

The Eastern Lodgings and Chapel of Okehampton Castle, as seen from the south-west.

Baldwin de Brionne, who was a son of the Count Gilbert of Brionne and a descendent of Duke Richard I of Normandy.

Baldwin was a powerful man and was in charge of controlling Devon and Cornwall after the conquest, when the Normans had pushed into the South West from Hastings. The Normans wanted complete control over the Saxons, but in order to defend themselves from uprisings by the Saxons, in which the people of Devon were involved in 1067, the Normans built castles. The Anglo-Saxon Chronicles of 1087 stated:

Castles William the Conqueror caused to be made, and the poor men to be greatly oppressed. The king was so very rigid, and took from his subjects a mark of gold, and more hundred pounds of silver, which he took, by weight and with great unright from his people, for little need. He has fallen into covetousness, and altogether loved greediness.

Baldwin de Brionne, as Sheriff of Devon, built a castle at Exeter in 1068, from where he administered over a huge area. Although it is unclear whether he actually gave the orders for Okehampton Castle to be constructed, it is clear that he owned it in 1086. He was a very rich man who had nearly 200 manors in Devon that had been taken from the local Saxon lords. The countryside was run by a distinct hierarchy. The king expected and received complete loyalty from Baldwin and he, in return, received lands and other favours. Baldwin gave a lot of his lands to his knights to maintain, who also became very rich. Below the knights were the soldiers who gained a living through loyalty to their lords and masters. Finally there were the Saxon peasants who continued to work the land as they had always done and therefore were not enormously affected by the changes.

In 1090 Baldwin died and was succeeded by his three sons, William, Robert and Richard. The brothers had interests all over the country including South Wales, after the Normans had invaded there, as well as back in Normandy. As such, they were not often living in Okehampton.

We know, however, that Richard, the last of Baldwin's sons, died in 1137 and there were no male heirs to take on the running of the castle and all the extensive estates. It appears that there had also been daughters and other women in Baldwin's family for it is the husbands of these women who owned the castle until 1173. That year Hawisia, the last heiress of the de Brionne family, married Reginald Courtenay. This marks the beginning of a long settled period when the castle is owned by the Courtenays, a local family who also owned a large number of manors in the borough of Okehampton. Later descendants of this family became the Earls of Devon – the present owners of Powderham Castle near Exeter – and were an extremely powerful force in the land. As the family owned a great many manors and large houses, they were not always living in the castle but rather on their estates.

At the end of the twelfth century most of the castles in this part of the West Country, such as Launceston and Okehampton, were maintained by King Richard I, who was afraid of a French invasion and indeed of his brother John!

The Courtenays had Okehampton Castle as the centre of their estates and wealth until 1538. Indeed it was the barony of Okehampton that gave them their family fortunes. Reginald, who had been the first of the Courtenays at Okehampton Castle, died in 1190 and his son Robert took on the responsibilities as landowner. He granted a borough charter to Okehampton in 1219. There then followed after his death in 1242, John Courtenay, then Hugh

Courtenay I, who died in 1292. Next came Hugh II, who succeeded when he was only sixteen years old. His earldom of Devon had lapsed so he was not created Earl of Devon until five years before his death in 1340.

The castle was rebuilt and enlarged in the fourteenth century and became more of a fortified manor-house than a castle. Also created at this time was a large deer park on the south side of the castle that runs up to the edge of the moor. (This was later desecrated by the infamous Okehampton bypass.)

The period 1377–1556 saw various generations of the Earls of Devon meet a variety of ends: some died of natural causes, others were killed, while some were imprisoned or executed. Such was life in the fourteenth and fifteenth centuries! One of the mistakes the Courtenays made was to be involved in the Wars of the Roses. Thomas Courtenay I supported the Yorkists and was tried for treason but he was pardoned in 1457, while Thomas II fought for Henry VI but was taken prisoner and beheaded in 1461 having had all his estates confiscated by the Crown. These were then given by Edward IV to a Humphrey Stafford who therefore, briefly, became Earl of Devon in 1469, before he was also executed! The see-saw fortunes and misfortunes of the Earls of Devon continued for several more decades from 1470 to 1509; one year the earls were in favour with the Crown, the next they were out of favour – which sometimes led to imprisonment and even execution.

In 1485 Henry Tudor must have looked favourably on the Courtenays as he returned all the Devon estates to the family. Despite this there were soon more problems, for in 1503 William Courtenay was imprisoned in the Tower for six years for plotting against the Crown. By 1539 there were still more upsets as William's son, Henry who had been made Marquis of Exeter in 1525 by Henry VIII, was eventually accused of conspiracy and was executed in 1539. Once again all the estates were confiscated by the Crown and Henry's son Edward was also put in prison. Edward was forgiven by Queen Mary in 1553 and was made Earl of Devon. He was later accused of being involved in a rebellion and fled the country. He died abroad in 1556. This period in the history of the Courtenay family is almost laughable if it was not so awful.

It is no wonder that the castle became run down during this period with leaking roofs, rotting timbers and crumbling walls. The Courtenays had really lost their power and no longer lived at Okehampton and consequently the castle fell into decay.

There are really no records showing what happened to the castle in the next period of history as it does not seem to have been involved in the Civil War of the seventeenth century. However in 1682 a certain John Ellacot, who later became Mayor of Okehampton, leased the castle and, I presume, lived there in what remained of the ruins that were habitable. He also used one of the buildings as a bakehouse. This is the first time that we hear of what happened to what had once been the proud home of a proud family. After that one can only assume that the castle became more and more ruined and became completely deserted; much of the building was dismantled in the sixteenth century. Sadly also a lot of the fabric and stones were taken to be used in other buildings.

More recently the castle was owned by Sydney Simmons a local benefactor who carried out considerable restoration work on the ruins. In 1917 he handed it over to the Okehampton Castle Trust who, in 1967, placed it in the guardianship of the Ministry of Public Buildings and Works. In 1984 English Heritage took it over. Between 1972 and 1980 considerable excavations were carried out and I shall be referring to some of the finds later on. Since then there has been a programme of maintenance and development.

The remains of the Keep as seen in June 1890.

Quite clearly Okehampton Castle was the central headquarters, if you like, of the new, noble, feudal landowners from where the administration of the lands took place. From Baldwin de Brionne to the Courtenays it was a symbol of authority, power and might; the new social elite. These people lived lavish lifestyles, entertaining with banquets, dancing and music. With the deer park just across the valley from the castle there would have been hunting parties with sumptuous feasts after the chase. Archaeologists have found an amazing number of different bones during their digs and from those they were able to see what the diet must have been like for the nobility. There were as you might expect pig, sheep and cattle bones and a huge number of bones of fallow deer, mainly the haunches. They also ate salmon and eel but a large number of fish bones were found; indeed most of the fish that we eat today. The list continues with the bones of hare, rabbit, chicken, goose, duck, pigeon, partridge, woodcock as well as waders and sea birds, and even the remains of oysters, whelks and mussels. With Okehampton being so far from the sea one cannot help wondering how fresh the sea fish was when it arrived.

The domestic arrangements for the running of the castle would have been in the hands of the lady of the house, while she had under her a large number of servants each dealing with different aspects of the work. There would also have been many stewards who were responsible for the running of the estates scattered around Devon and further afield. There was also a group of servants with the unusual name of the 'riding household'. They were employed to leave at very short notice with the Courtenays when they set off to visit their many large estates and stay at the manors scattered around the country. It was the duty of these servants to look after the comfort of the family on their travels and assure their welfare on arrival at their destination; they might well be away from Okehampton for many weeks at a time.

Although the castle was rebuilt in the fourteenth century and became more of a fortified residence and therefore could not have been taken easily by force, it was never, as far as we know, subject to any warfare and it was never besieged (although it had potential military importance). It was not even utilised during the Civil War. Its main importance was to remain an example of the feudal nobility's power, prestige and authority.

The excellent little guide produced by English Heritage which can be bought at the entrance booth takes you on a tour of the castle. Various areas of interest include:

1. **The Barbican.** This was a gatehouse, built at the end of a long narrow Barbican passage that led to the main entrance. It was here in the tunnel that any attackers could be constrained early in their forced entry.

2. **The Gatehouse.** At this main entrance there was a pit to allow a drawbridge to move up and down. The gatekeeper probably lived in a room on the first floor and from here he would have controlled the machinery for the drawbridge. To the right is another small room, an ante chamber, which could well have been a guard room or where lowly people waited before they were ushered into the Great Hall.

3. **The Great Hall.** This must have been a magnificent building of great height for it was open to the rafters and beams in the roof for most of its length. There are several windows and an entrance from the bailey court (a bailey is a defended courtyard of a castle) in the south wall. There are several sockets where massive timbers were located to support a wooden screen and the roof timbers. Two doors at the west end led to the kitchen and the service room, while a third opened on to a short staircase outside the hall on the north side. There are several ornate doorways and

The Great Hall, seen from near the entrance of the castle complex.

interestingly they all have slots for lengths of timber to be inserted as bars to keep people out. There is a fireplace in the west wall and in the north-west corner a latrine, known as a garderobe, with a shoot running into a drain.

Above left: The kitchen and Great Hall, as seen from the motte.

Above: Inside the Great Hall.

4. **The Kitchen.** A passage with a roof led to the Hall from the kitchen so that hot food would not cool on its way to the table. There are various rooms, one with a large granite hearth (where a great number of the bones I mentioned were excavated). Another room had a storage pit and two ovens. Smoke probably just drifted up to the roof of this room which seems to have been quite high. A lead water pipe was discovered to the south of these rooms, which collected water from the motte. Beneath another building at the foot of the motte a water cistern over 6ft deep was cut into the rock.

5. **The Motte.** This is a huge mound raised on the highest point of the spur which was the natural feature that dictated where the castle should first be built. It is made of shale, rock and other debris that was dug out from the ditches on the east and west sides. On the south side the natural rock forms part of the mound.

6. **The Keep.** The remains of the eleventh-century tower can still be made out at a lower level but a change of style and masonry shows that rebuilding took place in the fourteenth century. A staircase led up to the first floor

The motte and keep.

where there was a turret from which one could gain access to a parapet. A garderobe can still be seen in the south-west corner. Five corbels which supported the roof are still in place and in the south wall at the level of the first-floor room another garderobe is visible with shoots on the outside wall discharging on to the slopes of the motte.

7. **The Western Lodging.** This was an outstanding building at the west end of the chapel. It had thick walls and good foundations that were built with care using stone from outside the area such as aplite and sandstone from Beer. A garderobe can be seen in the south wall. The entrance was in the west wall. In the seventeenth century a great number of alterations took place; the entrance on the west side was blocked and a large oven was constructed which used a millstone as a base (suggesting that this part of the castle was used as a bakehouse). Two new entrances were made on both the south and the north sides, the latter having a porch. Various doors were blocked such as the medieval postern gate and the entrance to the priest's lodging but both of these have since been reopened. It must have been John Ellacot, who leased the castle in 1682, who carried out all these alterations while living there.

8. **The Priest's Lodging.** To the south of the chapel is a small building which was home to the priest appointed to the lord's family. He was able to enter his lodging through the chapel with another small entrance in the curtain wall.

9. **The Chapel.** The eastern end of the chapel still stands; it is possible to see remains of imitation red-painted joints on the south wall. Near here is a piscina. The corbels on the eastern wall may have been the supports for an altar and a statue above it. There are two windows which show signs of a Decorated Gothic style, common in England between 1290 and 1360. More corbels high up on the walls probably supported a sloping roof.

10. **The Eastern Lodgings.** Along with the Great Hall the three lodgings here are in a good state of preservation after extensive restoration work. These rooms for guests and important members of the household were all on the first floor. The lodgings were as comfortable as you could get in medieval times. There are several garderobes and in the one near the gatehouse you can see the slots for supporting a wooden seat and even a small stone washbasin. While the upper rooms were for VIPs quite clearly the lower rooms were also used, for there are garderobes here too.

One of the windows of the Chapel.

You might well have had enough wandering around the castle but it is worth following the Woodland Walk, which has numbered posts to guide you. It is an excellent nature trial and there are many species of flowers, trees, birds and animals to be seen at different times of the year. Again, a pamphlet is available.

It starts on the north-west side of the castle where in the sixteenth century a small stream was dammed to make a pond for fish; you may remember all the fish bones that were found, including bream, carp and roach. After a while you enter an area of woodland, some of which is very old, especially the oak trees which were used for coppicing while the mature trees were used in building and for ships. To your right is a ditch and a bank which might have been the remains of an earlier castle – possibly even from Saxon times.

The path starts to climb beside Reynard's Field. Fairly steep zig-zags take you down to the corner and there are glimpses across to the deer park from here. It was the Courtenay family who created the deer park in 1300 but not before they had moved several peasants out of their farms which were dotted about on the edge of the moor and were in the way of the park. The path turns back towards the castle and for a while you are quite close to the West Okement River. The hedge along here has been 'laid' – an old country method of cutting the trunks of small trees partially through and bending them down until they are horizontal and twining them together to form a dense barrier to restrain stock.

The Eastern Lodgings.

The final part of the walk takes you along the south-east edge of the castle below the postern gate, the Priest's Lodging and the Eastern Lodging. You will be able to make out the fireplaces and the garderobes with their shoots draining straight on to the embankment! Apparently the holes seen in the walls are where the wooden scaffolding was fixed during the building of the castle.

** You may not have time or indeed the inclination to have a further walk but I would like to recommend a route of about 4.5 miles/7.25km in which you will get a sense of more recent history.

I mentioned the narrow overgrown passage just by the car park for the castle that goes down to a footbridge over the West Okement River. Take that and it will lead you through woods and by fields to a right of way across

Okehampton Golf Course. Golf has taken the place of hunting in the deer park.

I am afraid you will have the constant roar of traffic along the controversial Okehampton bypass. As you can imagine plans to cut a dual-carriageway road through a National Park and a medieval deer park raised storms of protest in 1984 from all amenity organisations including the redoubtable Lady Sylvia Sayer, that champion of Dartmoor as well as of the Dartmoor Preservation Association and many others. Sylvia Sayer wrote, 'The history of Dartmoor itself is written in earth and stone across the landscape of the old deer park... it must surely be kept safe from planned devastation of any kind.' The alternative route would have been to the north of Okehampton through farm land, but this was opposed by local farmers who had on their side local MP Peter Mills who was himself a farmer. Nevertheless the bypass was built. Cynics claimed that more damage had been done to the Dartmoor National Park after it was made a National Park than before. Lady Sayer knighted her donkey, Rastus, after Peter Mills had also been knighted by the Queen!

The walk continues through fields and scrubland until a bridge takes you over the bypass and into a delightful wood by the river. You will arrive at the Meldon Viaduct. The London & South Western Railway Company opened a single line from Okehampton to Lydford in 1874, which eventually went to Tavistock and Bude. Lying in the way of the construction was the steep-sided valley of the West Okement River, so a viaduct was built across it. The viaduct spans nearly 540ft across the river and at the highest point is 150ft above the river. By the 1880s a second viaduct also carrying a railway track was built beside the existing one. Meldon Viaduct is now a Scheduled Ancient Monument as it is an example of wrought-iron truss-girder construction, of which there are only two in Britain.

In 1965 Beeching struck and the line to the north of Cornwall that took so much holiday traffic along the edge of the moor to Tavistock was closed. (Dr Beeching, who came from ICI, was appointed by the Government to look into the future of railways in Britain; he was to establish whether a line made a profit, regardless of any social or local business needs. He recommended that a large number of lines were closed, including a great many in the country-side, which left large areas of rural Britain without vital railway links.) In 1970 a concrete road was constructed across the viaduct to carry materials for the next place this walk visits, another disaster for Dartmoor National Park,

The Meldon Viaduct.

the Meldon Dam. By 1990 the rails had been taken up and the viaduct is now used by the National Cycle Network and, of course, by walkers.

Meldon Viaduct, from an old postcard.

Continue up the picturesque valley past a deep quarry lake on the other side of the river, where in my misguided youth, I used to dive with an aqualung amongst the old cars, fridges and other rubbish dumped there! As you round the corner you will see the huge wall of the 132ft-deep dam. It holds back 680 million gallons of water covering an area of 57 acres.

The damming of the steep-sided valley of the West Okement was suggested in 1962 when the North Devon Water Board stated that more water was needed to satisfy demand in the area. It was opposed by the National Park Committee and all the amenity societies and in March 1965 a public inquiry was held in Exeter. Sixteen months later the Water Board won, even though the planning assessor said that it was a mistake to build a dam in a National Park. He also said that a site at Gorhuish, outside the National Park, should be reconsidered as an alternative.

Meldon Dam.

The amenity societies took the matter to select committees in both Houses of Parliament in 1967. The committees said that they preferred the Gorhuish site but if it proved impracticable or much more expensive, then the dam at Meldon should go ahead. Traces of arsenic were found in the soil in the West Okement valley but in the long run this did not seem to cause any problems. The Water Board and the Ministry found that the cost of building the dam at Gorhuish was going to be 37 per cent more expensive than that at Meldon so permission to start work at Meldon was granted; it began in 1970. The reservoir was opened on 22 September 1972 by – yes, you've guessed it – Peter Mills MP! One can only assume from this outcome that the protection of a National Park was not worth the extra money it would have cost to build the dam elsewhere.

You can, if you are feeling strong, climb up to the left of the dam where you will find a path that leads you to a gate where you can gain access to the top of the dam. The view, of course, is impressive, as water always adds a beauty and a charm to a scene but should it be here? I leave it to you to decide.

Simply retrace your steps back to the castle. I feel that the views walking back on a route are still interesting – you see everything from a different angle.

Meldon Reservoir.

WALK 6

BRAT TOR, GREAT LINKS TOR, BLEAK HOUSE, RATTLEBROOK PEAT WORKS,
CORN RIDGE, BRANSCOMBE'S LOAF, SOURTON TORS, THE ICE WORKS.

**START: On the common near the Dartmoor Inn, Lydford.
Map ref.: 526853. Long. 8.5 miles/13.75 km. Moderate.
By leaving out Branscombe's Loaf and Sourton Tors the walk
can be reduced to 6 miles/9.75km.**

There is a lane north of the Dartmoor Inn that will take you through a gate to the open moor and to a car park. Please shut the gate. There are two pubs near the start of this walk: the Dartmoor Inn and, just up the road towards Okehampton, the Fox and Hounds, which could also make a starting point as there is a way on to the moor here at Nodden Gate. The map will show you how to link up with the route I shall be describing. Lydford is close with all the facilities of a small village.

Set off along the track by the fence which will then run slightly downhill, north-east to the River Lyd. There are three ways to get across the river: by the bridge, the stepping stones or by the ford. Before you cross over, walk down to your right along the river for around 200yds to see a sad reminder of the First World War. Here there is a seat and nearby a plaque, attached to a rock, that reads, 'In loving memory of Captain Nigel Duncan Ratcliffe Hunter, MC and Bar, Royal Engineers, who was killed in action near Bapaume, on March 25th 1918 aged 23 years.' This young man clearly loved Dartmoor and on the plaque you will also find a short, poignant poem written by him on his last visit to Lydford.

The three ways over the River Lyd.

Return to the bridge and take the smaller, steep path to the right of the main track that runs up to **Brat Tor** and Widgery Cross, which you will see on the skyline. The views from Widgery Cross are wonderful as they look out across North Devon, down to Cornwall and away into the heart of the moor. When you arrive there, no doubt panting a bit – it is quite steep – you will see that this well-known cross is made of small blocks of granite rather than being carved from one piece as are many of the other ancient Dartmoor crosses. It stands some 13ft high and was erected in 1887 at the instigation of W. Widgery, the Dartmoor artist, to celebrate the golden jubilee of Queen Victoria. William Widgery painted over 3000 pictures in his lifetime (not all of Dartmoor) and had no difficulty in selling them and indeed his pictures of Dartmoor are still very much sought after. He captured the soft, misty landscape of the moor with its gentle, pastel shades of colour and gaunt, black tors.

Widgery Cross.

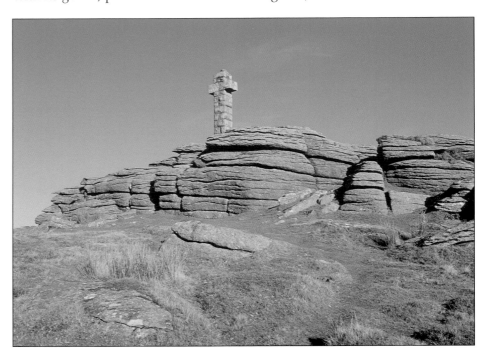

Widgery was born in South Molton in 1822 and had no formal art training. He went abroad and painted in Italy and Switzerland. He then found inspiration in the Devon and Cornwall coasts before turning his attention to

Dartmoor and becoming one of the key painters connected with the moor. He was primarily a landscape artist, as was his son Frederick, born in 1861.

Aim north-north-east, just to the right of Arms Tor which you will see straight ahead. You will come to the miners' track that you could have followed from the bridge over the River Lyd if you had wished to miss out Widgery Cross. You will be in an area of tinners' spoil heaps, gerts and gullies. Opposite the deep gert to your left is Dick's Well, which is the source of the Doetor Brook.

As the track begins to swing north you will see, to your left, the two tors called Higher Dunna Goat and Lower Dunna Goat with **Great Links Tor** beyond with its Trig Point. These two tors, that lie more on the side of the hill than on the top, have strange names; they have nothing to do with goats but derive from the Celtic words 'dan' meaning under (or possibly 'dun' meaning a hill) and 'coed' meaning a wood. Trees certainly grew to this height in early times.

There is nothing to be gained by climbing up to the two tors as you will miss a chance to poke about in the ruins of **Bleak House** which lies on the far side,

'The Tavy Cleave' by F.J. Widgery.

Bleak House.

the left bank, of the Rattle Brook. This is a splendidly apt name for this lonely and remote ruin, home to the manager of the peat works we are going to visit. Eden Phillpotts knew about this house and described it in his novel *The Whirlwind*, in which he called it Dunnagoat Cottage. He wrote:

Peat cutting, 1912.

> *... they approached a solitary grey cottage that stood naked in the very heart of the wilderness. Stark space surrounded it. At first sight it looked no more than a boulder, larger than common, that had been hurled hither from the neighbouring hill at some seismic convulsion of olden days. But, unlike the stones around it, this lump of lifted granite was hollow, had windows pierced in its lowly chambers, and a hearth upon its floor. It seemed a thing lifted by some sleight of power unknown, for it rose here utterly unexpected, and, as it appeared, without purpose. Heather-clad ridges of peat ran to the very threshold; rough, natural clitters of rock tumbled to its walls; doors and windows opened upon primal chaos, rolling and rising, sinking and falling in leagues on every side.*

Keep walking north up the valley of Rattle Brook and you will soon come to the extensive industrial areas of the **Rattlebrook Peat Works**. This is a desolate, almost ugly place, although nature has helped to soften what man has done to his environment. The peat works was one of the few old industries that survived on Dartmoor until 1955 when the venture was finally closed down.

A peat cutter's shovel.

Cutting peat to use as fuel is nothing new on Dartmoor; a charter in the times of Henry III granting people the right to cut peat refers to it as coal. The smoke of burning peat has an almost indefinable smell that you only get now in the remote parts of Ireland. The tinners had rights to take peat and it was used in their mines. However, it burns rapidly and therefore charcoal was preferred. Everyone who lived on Dartmoor used it as a fuel in their homes and farms and every dwelling had a stack of peat outside. In the eighteenth century there was quite a trade taking dried peat turves down to the South Hams to be sold for a 1s. (10p) a dozen. The Revd John Swete, who you will remember from Walk 3, noted that he had seen a man cut 'fat, bitumous turf' and then trudge 6 miles into Tavistock to sell 20 slabs for 2s., which seems to have been the going price.

Each peat slab was 20in. long, 7in. wide and 2in. thick. A good peat cutter would cut 1440 slabs in half a day, which would then be piled up in pairs behind the cutting area to dry. The section of the moor where peat was cut was called a tie and was about 40yds long. A tie would probably last a farmer about twenty years. It is interesting that workers at Rattlebrook cut a slightly smaller slab but their tie was 60yds. They talked about completing a journey when they came to end of the tie. The pay was usually half a crown (22½p) a journey.

It was discovered that naphtha, petrol, tar oil and acetic acid could be extracted from peat and this brought a glint into the eye of quite a number of entrepreneurs. The first and in some ways the most successful business was set up in 1844 with a sum of £19 000, which in those days was a huge amount of money. A distillation plant was set up at Bachelor's Hall near Princetown and as the prison was empty at the time, the industry was moved there. Based in the prison's infirmary buildings, the British Patent Naphtha Company produced gas as well as candles made from naphtha and moth balls. Such candles burn with a very bright, white flame and were popular for use in the mines by the tinners. Other peat ventures sprung up all over Dartmoor but most failed after only a few years.

The iron head of a peat cutter's shovel, found on Dartmoor.

At Rattlebrook, however, the thought of fortunes to be made from naphtha attracted speculators to the vast peat beds, as yet untapped, up high on Dartmoor. In 1878 The West of England Compressed Peat Company, made up mainly from businessmen from Exeter, decided to employ an invention by a John Howard from Topsham that compressed peat by a hydraulic machine and extracted the water. This venture failed after only two years.

By 1879 a railway line had been built, with something of the same skill as the engineers who built the Foggintor and Swelltor Quarries Railway that eventually went to Princetown. Trains carried the dried peat down to the main line of the old London & South Western Railway which ran over Meldon Viaduct (Walk 5) to Bridestowe; you can still see the disused linking tracks and sidings. The climb up to the works was over 1000ft; it was an extraordinary feat of engineering. You will follow sections of this moorland track for part of this walk.

In 1901 another company took over Rattlebrook with the plan to carbonise the peat. This also proved to be unsuccessful. Then a German arrived claiming to have invented a way of extracting alcohol from peat; unfortunately he is said to have died without letting anybody know his secret formula! The belief persisted that from peat it was possible to extract crude oils, petrol and gas and

The old railway line leading from Rattlebrook Peat Works.

yet another company took on Rattlebrook in 1937 and built a plant there for this purpose. An even more unlikely speculator arrived who wanted to build a spa up here in order to give patients peat baths. His idea was to upgrade the disused railway running from Bridestowe and bring his customers up by comfortable carriages to wallow in hot, brown peaty water! The war put pay to that venture.

After the Second World War, in 1946, peat was once again being cut. In 1955 peat taken from Rattlebrook was used for horticultural and agricultural purposes for a firm in Torquay. Some of this peat was used in 1956 at the Royal Show for use as bedding for flowers and shrubs. Transport costs finally made extracting peat uneconomical. In 1961 the Army was ordered to demolish all the disused buildings, as part of an exercise. Rattlebrook is once again empty, remote and full of ghosts. So ended another Dartmoor industry, just like George Templer's enterprise at Haytor Quarries (Walk 1).

The ruins of Rattlebrook Peat Works.

If you want to shorten the walk, there is a gentle route down the old railway line that will lead you back to the start (north initially and then south-west and finally south past Great Nodden). Or, if you prefer, go to where the infant

River Lyd flows under the track, just over a mile from Rattlebrook, and you can follow that down to the start past amazing tinners' works. Keep an eye out for the tinners' cache, like a little cave, quite close to the river after you have left the railway track.

However, if you have the time there are more Dartmoor legends to hear about and history to discover. Climb more or less north to the little rock of Hunt Tor and then north-east to Woodcock Hill and finally **Corn Ridge**. Once on the plateau you should aim north-west towards Branscombe's Loaf. The views to your right are very exciting. The slope down to the West Okement, the river that flows past Okehampton Castle, is one of the steepest on Dartmoor. Below, but you will not see them unless you climb down, are the Slipper Stones, huge blocks of granite that are said to resemble giant slippers. On the far side of the valley lies Black-a-Tor Copse, one of the moor's three ancient oak woods, while above it rears Yes Tor and High Willhays – the highest peaks of Dartmoor.

Walk to **Branscombe's Loaf**. The name Loaf may come from the fact that the tor looks like a loaf of bread – and the smaller rock nearby is often called the Cheese! However, Loaf could be a corruption of the Celtic word 'llof', meaning a lump or excrescence. However, there is yet another possible explanation. As man has lived on Dartmoor since prehistoric times and as the landscape itself is often magical and mysterious it is no wonder that there are many legends and folk tales to be heard. Many of them, of course, are an attempt to explain some feature of the moor or to give an explanation to some unaccountable occurrence. Not surprisingly perhaps, many of the stories are linked to the Devil. In medieval times the parish of Lydford covered a huge area and the people of the moor had to worship and bury their dead at Lydford; they often carried the bodies on the back of a horse along the Lich Way, one of Dartmoor's ancient tracks. When they got near Lydford at the appropriately named Coffin Wood they put the body in a coffin to carry it the last few miles for burial. However in 1260 Walter Bronsecombe, Bishop of Exeter, allowed the people of the ancient tenements of Babeny, Pizzwell and Brimpts to worship and bury their dead in Widecombe-in-the-Moor. One day Bishop Bronsecombe was lost on the moor, but much to his relief, an old man appeared who looked like a moorman and offered him some bread and cheese. He was just about to accept when he saw a cloven hoof sticking out from beneath the moorman's cloak. It was the Devil in disguise! The Bishop threw down the loaf of bread and the piece of cheese, both of which turned instantly to stone as you can see for yourselves!

From Branscombe's Loaf walk down past a cairn, a Bronze-Age burial mound, towards the north. You might just stumble on a large stone circle but with many stones missing it is difficult to see. It is quite close to where a reave (an ancient earth-and-stone boundary bank) crosses a track.

Aim straight at *Sourton Tors*, still to the north-west or follow the track round, which you would cross in any case, to the tors. To your right, as your line of vision goes beyond the spur of Shelstone Tor north of Branscombe's Loaf, you will see Meldon Reservoir tucked in its steep valley. On the north side of Sourton Tors you will see a strange series of bumps, pits, mounds and ruined buildings. These were once the *Ice Works*. Water was run into the shallow pits that you can see and on frosty days it froze. The ice was then cut out and stored in specially dug trenches waiting to be transported to Plymouth by horse and cart for use by the fishermen and fishmongers. This venture was started in 1875 and lasted about ten years. The position here is ideal; it is high on the moor and north-facing, in line with freezing winter winds. What a business, taking the ice down to Plymouth by horse and cart; I wonder how much melted on the journey. Another failed Dartmoor industry!

Return to the track and follow it round and then south. Keep on it past the reave and past Lake Down and Coombe Down. Here you will join the disused track of the peat railway that you must keep following under Great Nodden where there is an amazing series of tracks, sidings and evidence of points.

To your right you will see King Wall and, running beside it, the King Way, an ancient track that leads to Nodden Gate. This was the old route along the north-west side of Dartmoor that became disused when the stagecoach roads were built in the eighteenth century. Keep on the tracks by a wall running beside a river, until you come to the bridge back over the River Lyd and the climb back to the car park.

WALK 7

LYDFORD CASTLE AND THE CHURCH OF ST PETROCK

START: Car park (with public conveniences) opposite the pleasant-looking pub, The Castle, and nearly opposite the castle. Map ref.: 510847. Short. 0.5 mile. Easy.

As you drive through the village you will see The Old Post Office. The new Post Office is back on the main Okehampton to Tavistock road situated in a garage, where you may choose to buy refreshments. Alternatively, you could visit the Dartmoor Inn on the opposite side of the road (which you drove past to the start of Walk 6).

Lydford Castle.

Commemorating the Viking invasion that was repulsed in AD997, the plaque behind the stone was erected in 1997 and reads: 'Vikings AD997–1997. This stone was raised when the men from the North came again, this time in peace. ERIK the Red carved the runes.'

It is hard to imagine that Lydford was probably one of the most important small towns in Devon; it is a quiet backwater nowadays. As I have suggested elsewhere, location is key to the establishment of a new settlement, and Lydford is situated on triangular, high ground between two gorges of the River Lyd and one of its tributaries. As such, it could be easily defended. Celtic people probably settled here first; pottery from the Mediterranean has been discovered on archaeological digs. It could have been a frontier post to guard against the Britons who came on raids over the Cornish border. Indeed there is record of a battle being fought at Galford not so far away. There is even a strange but unfounded claim that Julius Caesar visited Lydford. (I am not sure as to the roots of this claim, as the Romans did not really penetrate this far west.)

It seems that the first known reference to Lydford occurs in the tenth-century list known as the Burghal Hidage. Here it was described as a fortified town or burh in the Saxon Kingdom of Wessex ruled over by King Alfred. It was at this time that the Vikings were invading Britain in their longships and as the Anglo-Saxon Chronicles of AD997 puts it, they were: 'Turning into the mouth of the Tamar, the Vikings went up till they came to Lideford, burning and slaying everything they met'. On the way to Lydford they pillaged and burnt the Benedictine abbey at Tavistock which had been founded twenty-three years before. To protect his burh, King Alfred built timber walls on two sides of the town and dug ditches and raised earth ramparts on the third – it is still possible to see this today, referred to as Town Bank, on the way out of the village towards the main road. The Burghal Hidage mentions that four men were needed to maintain and defend the wall every 5½yds. It obviously worked for the Vikings were defeated and withdrew back to their ships.

By the late-tenth century Lydford was the largest parish in Devon and was one of Devon's five boroughs. Both tin and silver were mined locally and there was a royal mint here, one of four in Devon. Silver coins were struck – the Lydford Pennie. The most famous perhaps is a coin of Ethelred II (c.969–1016) which is now in the British Museum. You can also see examples of these silver pennies, that were issued for over seventy years, in the Castle Inn. Interestingly, when the Vikings sacked the abbey at Tavistock and tried to take Lydford, they must have stolen quite a number of the Lydford Pennies for many are held in Scandinavian museums!

By the Middle Ages most of the administration for the Royal Forest of Dartmoor came from Lydford. It was also the centre for running the stannaries for the Devon tin-mining industry. In spite of all this Lydford suffered a depression for in 1195 King Richard I ordered the lord of the manor to open up the town's market again, which must have closed, set up a stannary court and erect a stone keep known as Lydford Castle to hold the King's prisoners; it cost £74 to build.

Lydford Castle became the stannary court as well as the court for those who had broken the harsh forest laws. Forest, you will remember, referred to the royal hunting lands of the kings. The castle was also the prison where those who were convicted of breaking both forest and stannary laws were held. It had a terrible and notorious reputation for handing out rigorous punishment. In 1644 William Browne wrote what was considered a humourous 20-verse poem called 'A Lydford Journey'. It starts:

The interior of Lydford Castle, with the dungeon entrance on the right, photographed in 1890.

> *I oft have heard of Lydford law,*
> *How in the morn they hang and draw,*
> *And sit in judgement after:*
> *At first I wonder'd at it much;*
> *But now I find their reason such,*
> *That it deserves no laughter.*

It was meant to be written as a joke but it was, in fact, not far from the truth as the tyranny was terrible in the early days. Even during the reign of Henry VIII an Act described Lydford prison as, 'one of the most annoious, contagious and detestable places within this realme'.

There is an interesting little bit of history that emerges concerning a Richard Strode who was a tinner and an MP. He was thrown into the dungeon at Lydford for daring to promote a bill in the Houses of Parliament that was to control the pollution of streams and rivers by mine waste. However, his imprisonment paid off in the end for in 1509 an Act was passed that gave freedom of speech and discussion on any subject in Parliament.

Even the notorious Judge Jeffreys was said to have sat in judgement at Lydford Castle in the time of James II and we all know his reputation. Almost as if to get their own back on him, villagers have claimed that Lydford was haunted by him in the shape of a black pig!

What you see here is the medieval castle on its mound which was used, as I have said, both as courtroom and a prison until the eighteenth century. With the building of Princetown Prison during the Napoleonic Wars to take French prisoners of war in the early-nineteenth century, Lydford's prison was no longer needed – after the wars, when the French left, English prisoners were held at Princetown instead.

There were two building periods of this castle. The first, as you read earlier, was when the lord of the manor was instructed to build a keep in 1195 by Richard I. These lower walls of the original keep are now sunk deep in the present mound which was piled up and built later against the old walls. On top of these original walls, now really foundations, are the walls built in the thirteenth century when the castle was rebuilt. On the other side of the castle from the road there was a courtyard, also constructed in the thirteenth century, which would have been surrounded by walls but now only the outline is extant, with earth banks showing where it once stood. This area would have included various buildings such as storerooms and stables.

The banks surrounding the old courtyard of Lydford Castle.

The entrance to the castle is also on the side away from the road. As a consequence of the mound being raised later, once you are inside the keep you will go down to the original ground level. The walls were enormously thick – over 10ft. There was no entrance in the early keep at ground level and only narrow slits for windows. In the thirteenth century the old keep and gaol (except the lower parts of the walls) were demolished, so nobody knows what the upper storeys were like nor indeed how many floors had been built. It was around this time that the mound against the old walls was built up. Much thinner walls were then constructed on top of the old ones and the interior was filled with earth to the level of the new entrance to help strengthen the whole structure. English Heritage, who now manages the castle on behalf of the owner, the Duchy of Cornwall, removed this filling except in one corner.

It seems that in the thirteenth century Lydford Castle was used only as a prison for the door was locked from the outside. There was one cell at a lower level, a sort of dungeon, below ground level and another cell at what was the new ground level of the mound. There is another door to the left that could well have been some private room where an official had his offices. The two windows suggest that there was another floor above here where two rooms were reached by the stairs set into the wall to the right of the door. This quite clearly was better accommodation where the lord or constable of the castle lived. There are stone benches below the windows and fireplaces. As was seen at Okehampton Castle there were garderobes (latrines) set into the thick walls.

One of Lydford Castle's cell windows.

All is in an excellent state of preservation and it is easy to imagine the wretched prisoners awaiting their fate, probably hanging, locked in this ancient and notorious castle.

It is worth noting that there was a Norman castle near this site before the medieval one was built. If you would like to have a look at that then go back to the road and you will see a gate on your right that leads between the castle and the churchyard. Walk around the churchyard until you come to the end of the promontory on which Lydford is built. You will see a hedge to your right that marks the limits of the original Saxon ramparts as well as timber walls and ditches that were built to keep the Vikings out. The site of these defences was well chosen as the slope below falls steeply away to the gorge.

On the top of the steepest part of the slope was the site for the Norman castle that was built just after the Normans invaded Britain at the end of the eleventh century. It was not much of a castle compared to others built around the same time elsewhere in Britain, including that at Okehampton. Although the old Saxon defences were utilised, including, of course, the steep slope of the gorge, the walls were only timber with battlemented tops and earth dug out from a ditch piled up against them. This earth reinforcement was to resist attack by enemies wielding battering rams.

There would have been a small wooden gatehouse to guard the entrance to the wooden castle. Within the walls archaeological digs have found the remains of five small buildings that were built of wood and cob. Used in the construction of many old Devon houses, cob involves mixing mud with straw and plastering it onto a framework of laths until it is many feet thick. After it has been rendered and limewashed, as the castle buildings were, a strong, insulating wall is produced that lasts many years. The small houses in the castle were probably used as storerooms. Once the much stronger stone keep of Lydford Castle was built in 1195 there was probably no point in maintaining the wooden Norman castle and by the early 1200s it was abandoned and left to rot. All that is seen now are the grassy banks.

Walk back to the road and enter the churchyard. It may seem strange to have a church dedicated to a Cornish saint in Devon but **St Petrock** or Petroc was a great missionary and travelled all over the two counties, with his monks, preaching. There are at least 27 churches dedicated to him in Devon and Cornwall and even two in South Wales. It was said that he was

The ditch and ramparts of the old Norman castle at Lydford.

a Welsh prince who had turned his back on his royal upbringing and set off to study religion in Ireland, that other country of Celtic saints. While he was there he had a vision which told him to travel to Cornwall. He set sail from Ireland and after a rough voyage across the Irish Sea landed at the estuary of Camel in the sixth century. He settled there and built his first church at Lanwethinoc, which became Padstow. Later he moved on and founded a monastery at a place called Nanceventon, now Little Petherick, and a third and most important one at Bodmin. During this time he travelled around Devon and Cornwall (although it is even said that he visited Rome, Jerusalem and India) founding churches, including the one in the Celtic settlement of Lydford. Many legends about him survive; of how he turned water into nectar and tamed the terrible dragon that was plundering the Cornish countryside. He tied his stole round its neck and took it down to the sea near Padstow from where it swam away and vanished over the horizon never to be seen again! He converted Prince Constantine to Christianity and forced him to spend his life in poverty and prayer in a cell near the bay named after him in Cornwall. Like the Celtic peninsula of Cornwall with all its saints, Brittany also has a great many saints as seen by the names of the villages and towns there. Indeed St Petrock had contacts there and was well known in Brittany and much admired for his work.

St Petrock became a hermit and spent the end of his life as a recluse meditating near Bodmin. He died about AD564 at Treravel. His relics that were initially held at Bodmin were sold to the abbey in Meen, Brittany, by a renegade monk in 1177. However there was a great outcry and King Henry II, Overlord of Brittany, took charge and ordered that the relics should be returned to Bodmin in a gold and ivory casket. This was done but the relics have since disappeared. The casket, however, can still be seen in the church at Bodmin.

The first Saxon church founded by this saint who brought Christianity to Lydford in the sixth century, was probably made of wood. By 1237, just after Lydford Castle was built, there is reference to a stone church with a chancel and a nave. This was enlarged and rebuilt in 1261. In the forty years following 1428 the church was again enlarged and partly rebuilt with a south aisle, porch and a tower being added. However it is possible to see the remains of the earlier church; you can make out the old walls in the chancel and in the west wall of the nave.

Lydford's castle and church, from an old print.

When you wander around the outside of the church, go to the base of the tower and you will see that it was built 2ft away from the west wall. This was so that the congregation was able to keep using the church during the construction without too much disruption. When it was finished the tower was joined to the nave by a 'neck', which you can clearly see on both sides of the building. A tower buttress also had to be shortened so the joining wall could be put into position. An arch was put in so that people could get into the tower, which was made of huge blocks of Dartmoor granite, as indeed was

Lydford's Church of St Petrock.

the rest of the church. When it was first built the tower had four storeys with the bell-ringers' chamber on the first floor. However, this floor was dismantled so that the ringers could stand on the ground floor. Originally there were five bells that were recast using additional metal from three much older bells in 1789. A sixth bell was bought and hung in 1921 to improve the peal. The louvres of the belfry are made of stone.

Much of what you see inside the church dates from the end of the nineteenth and early-twentieth centuries. A pamphlet you can obtain as you enter the building gives details of the various points of interest in the church. Some of the old fabric is still visible such as the north wall of the chancel, dating from 1261, and the lancet window near the vestry. Near the altar that was made of oak in 1923, there are memorial stones in the floor. One is to Mrs Elizabeth Farrington who had eight knights in her family. Another remembers the Revd T. Burnaford who instigated repairs and restoration between 1701 and 1740.

In the nave, if you look high up on the west wall, you will see the remains of a window that dates from 1261, which was demolished to get into the tower.

Most of the stained glass is Victorian, as is so often the case in our churches, but there are a few examples of older glass. There is a window in the south-west wall that was put in during 1887 when the priest's door was blocked, but it also includes some pieces of old glass. The roundels are said to be fifteenth-century Flemish showing St Catherine of Siena to the left and St Anne on the right. Other pieces of old glass depict the virgin and child; supposedly this glass came form Salisbury Cathedral.

Left: *The Flemish glass in this window in Lydford's church dates from the fifteenth century.*

Below: *The church is also home to a pre-Norman font made of Hurdwick stone and set on a granite base.*

The lead-lined font in the nave is made from a block of Hurdwick stone standing on a granite base and is probably pre-Norman. It is one of only three tub-shaped fonts in Devon. There is evidence that the font once had a lid to prevent people from stealing the holy water; there are the remains of a hinge and staple on the rim dating from about 1216. The nave also includes pews with carved ends that were put in during 1923–26. The scenes depict 'The prophets, martyrs, The holy Catholic Church throughout the world and the Holy and Humble men of Heart'. On the ends of the second pew from the back, on the north side of the main aisle, St Edward the Confessor and St Dunstan can be found. These were donated by the late Duke of Windsor when he was Duke of Cornwall.

The watchmaker's tomb.

Whilst at the church, it is worth finding the watchmaker's tomb near the porch on the right. It reads:

Here lies in horizontal position
The outsize case of
GEORGE ROUTLEDGE, Watchmaker
Whose abilities in that line were an honour
To his profession
Integrity was the mainspring,
And prudence the regulator
Of all actions of his life.
Human, generous and liberal
His hand never stopped
Till he had relieved distress.
So much regulated were all his motions
That he never went wrong
Except when set agoing
By people
Who did not know
His key.
Even then he was easily
Set right again.
He had an art of disposing his time
So well
That his hours glided away
In one continual round
Of pleasure and delight
Till an unlucky minute put a period to
His existence.
He departed this life
Nov. 14 1802
Aged 57
Wound up
In hopes of being taken in hand
By his Maker
And of being thoroughly cleaned, repaired
And set-going
In the world to come.

Apparently this epitaph was first published in 1797 in an almanac produced by an American scholar named Benjamin Banneker and was borrowed by the friends and family of George Routledge.

If you can wind up your energy and spring along past the Castle Inn there are just a few more sites that might interest you before you leave Lydford. At the start of this walk, I mentioned the defences put up by Alfred in Saxon times and the Town Bank at the north-east end of the village. If you walk up the main street you will see the Bank on either side at the end of the village where it would have blocked the entrance to the promontory. It is extraordinary to think that it has survived when you consider that it was constructed two centuries before the Normans arrived and built their castle. Archaeologists have found that originally the defences were made up of turves and saplings with a wooden wall on the outer edge but at a later date the wooden wall was replaced with granite blocks and a mound of soil and stones. These ramparts surrounded the whole of Alfred's burh with the gorge dropping away on the west, south and east sides beyond it; this was a remarkably good defensive position.

Lydford declined in importance so that by 1300 it only had 48 burgesses whereas Totnes for example had 380. By 1660 it was described as being 'a mean and miserable village consisting of about 20 houses.' This means that the present-day village, remarkably, is still based on the original plans and defences of a Saxon burh with a main street crossed at right angles by three parallel side streets and surrounded by ramparts.

You can return to the car park by following a path that runs inside the ramparts to your left, on the north-west side of the main street. There is an interesting link back to Walk 6. William Widgery and his son Frederick lived in the house that is now Lydford House Hotel near the famous gorge. If you have time and need a bit more exercise then you could visit the famous and beautiful Lydford Gorge owned and managed by the National Trust. Just below the village, the gorge is, and has been for over three hundred years, one of the exciting tourist attractions in Devon. In the seventeenth century Tristram Risdon wrote that, 'it may be numbered amongst the wonders of this kingdom'.

The name Lyd is an Anglo-Saxon word meaning 'roaring stream' or 'torrent' and that is a perfect description of what you will find in the gorge, especially

The White Lady Waterfall at Lydford.

after rain. In 1630 a Thomas Westcote wrote, 'such a rumbling noise that it striketh a certain fear and terror to most strange passengers'. In the eighteenth century it was fashionable for young travellers to visit Lydford Gorge and marvel at the picturesque landscape and natural beauty. Artists also came to paint the dramatic scenery and our old friend the Revd John Swete painted a lovely picture of the cataract on the Lyd and later Frederick Widgery made a watercolour painting of the gorge.

It is a remarkable place with its ravines and whirlpools, its wildlife (it is a Site of Special Scientific Interest) and the White Lady Waterfall, Tunnel Falls, The Devil's Cauldron and Kitt's Steps. Legend has it that a Kitty Lampiere, coming back from a feast in Lydford on horseback, fell asleep on the panniers. She awoke to find herself hanging on the panniers with her horse struggling in the water below her. We do not known if she got out alive.

There are two entrances that are connected by a circular walk. The main entrance has a short walk to the Devil's Cauldron, while the other, the waterfall entrance, leads to the White Lady Waterfall. The gorge is open during the summer but in winter it is only open as far as the White Lady. At all times the route can be slippery but especially in winter so take care and wear good walking boots or shoes.

☞

WALK 8

The Church of St Michael, Brentor.

**START: Car park (with pubic conveniences) below the church.
Map ref.: 469805 on Landranger Sheet 201 or Explorer 112.**

There are various ways to get here. You can approach from Tavistock or from Mary Tavy, or indeed drive on past Lydford Gorge after Walk 7 and you will soon reach Brentor. The pleasant Brent Tor Inn is about 0.5 mile north-east of the tor, while nearby Tavistock has all the usual amenities of a small town.

It is fun to find links between the walks; for example, the Revd John Swete certainly seems to crop up quite often. There is, however, a link here between Brent Tor and Lydford Gorge. Thomas Fuller writing in about 1650 claimed:

We call the shavings of fish (which are little worth) gubbings; and sure it is they are sensible that the word importeth shame and disgrace. I have read of an England beyond Wales; but the Gubbings-land is a Scythia within England, and they pure heathens therein. It lieth nigh Brent-Tor, in the edge of Dartmoor. It is reported, that some two hundred years since, two strumpets being with child, fled thither to hide themselves, to whom certain lewd fellows resorted, and this was their first original.

It appears that in the sixteenth century a hoard of red-bearded Gubbinses terrified the area. Living in hovels in Lydford Gorge, which you may have visited during Walk 7, they seem to have been the Doones of Dartmoor. As the Revd Baring-Gould wrote, they survived by 'stealing sheep and cattle, and carrying them into the labyrinth of glens where they could not be traced. Charles Kingsley also used the story of the Gubbinses in *Westward Ho!* This group was a family of outlaws living in the gorge, killing, robbing and cattle

The Church of St Michael at Brentor.

rustling. Their leader was killed, as the story goes, in the Dartmoor Inn near the start of Walk 6, after which it is said, 'interbreeding and intemperance wiped them out'.

The Church of St Michael stands high above you as you cross the road from the car park, go through the gate and join the obvious track that climbs the hill. St Michael is traditionally the saint of high places, where he is said the have defeated evil. The embodiment of evil in paintings of this triumph has often been depicted as a dragon lunging out at him from swirling clouds.

There are over 800 churches dedicated to St Michael in England. The most well known is probably St Michael's Mount in Cornwall where fishermen are supposed to have seen St Michael in a vision in AD495. A chapel, dedicated to St Michael, was built in the castle on the summit. Across in Normandy, of course, there is the famous abbey at Mont St Michel. Back in Cornwall at Roche there are the remains of a chapel and a hermitage built in 1409 on the top of a huge rock that stands over 100ft high. There is also a ruined chapel on the summit of the hill at Glastonbury dedicated to St Michael. Some people believe that a 'ley line' links that chapel with St Michael's here at Brentor.

As you walk up the track with the rock and the church looming above you it becomes obvious that this terrain was once a volcanic lava flow. The igneous mass of Dartmoor oozed up in a great domed laccolith but the steep-sided abruptness of Brentor and the type of rock gives away its origins.

The name is something of a mystery. There is no mention of Brentor in the Domesday Book but by 1155 in the hamlet of Lideltona, now Liddaton, mention is made in a charter of Brenta. It has been suggested that Brent Tor actually means Burnt Tor, derived from the Saxon verb 'brennan' meaning to burn. However, the Saxon people would not have seen the lava erupting nor indeed if there had been a fire at one time here the burnt look of the moorland would soon disappear and fauna would grow again. It seems possible that the name comes from the Celtic word 'bryn' which means 'a hill' and another Celtic word

The Church of St Michael, Brentor.

'twr' which means 'a pile or heap of rocks'. Perhaps the name is 'bryn twr', the Celtic derivation meaning a 'hill crag'. This use of Celtic place names in the area is reflected in the name of a farm just south of Brentor, called Brinsabach. 'Bach' in Celtic, and in Welsh, means 'little', so the farm is named 'little hill'.

Walk up the slope and you will soon be aware of a low bank on your left. As you get higher, the track forks and if you follow round to your left into a gully you will see a low wall. These are the remains of the ramparts of another Iron-Age fort or castle. Return to the main track that climbs gently to the church and away below you, to your left, a rampart circles round all the way along the bottom of the hill; massive and impressive earthworks built between 150BC and AD50. This is another ancient monument that was excavated by Lady Aileen Fox whose name, you will remember, has cropped up on several other archaeological digs mentioned on previous walks. If you cast your mind back to the Iron-Age castles above the Teign, one cannot help but admire the incredible defensive positions that were occupied by Iron-Age people.

In Walk 7 we heard about St Petrock bringing Christianity to Lydford and founding a small chapel there. High places were considered sacred by both

A rampart of the Iron-Age fort at Brentor.

pagans and Christians, and indeed Christians often built their churches on the sites of pagan temples. It is therefore quite possible that some sort of religious building had long been present on the the rock but it was not until about 1130 that we get definite proof of a church on the tor. In the claiming of land in the deeds of Woburn a Walter Giffard wrote to Richard, Earl of Devon, saying:

My father, Robert Giffard, gave the Rock of Brentor to God, St Mary and the church of Tavistock as a perpetual gift, also thirty acres of his land at Lamerton, and the church of St Michael which he built on that same Rock at his own expense.

The church at Brentor, c.1890.

The Church of St Michael de Rupe (of the Rock) has several legends associated with its construction. One of these claims that originally the church was meant to be built at the foot of the tor. Work started there but every night the Devil carried all the stones to the top. Next day the builders carried the stones down again and started the foundations once more but sure enough when night came, the Devil took them all the way back to the top! Eventually, the legend has it, the builders got fed up with carting the stones down each day so they let the Devil have his own way and built the church on the top of the tor. It is an amusing thought that perhaps the Devil wanted the church on the top so that it would be difficult for people to come and worship – which indeed it is on stormy days, as you will read later!

Another legend has it that a wealthy merchant was caught in a terrible and ferocious storm out in the Channel beyond Plymouth Sound. It looked as if his ship was about to sink so he went down on his knees on the heaving deck and prayed, saying that he would build a church on the first land he sighted if his life was saved. Brentor is quite a long way from Plymouth Sound and the Channel so I rather doubt if the merchant would have seen the tor before anything else, unless the lower part of the land was covered with fog. However, that is the order of events according to the legend – and I must not cast doubt on such a splendid tale! A dramatic poem was written about it by Carrington:

Then
As bent timbers of his stout-ribb'd bark
To the huge ocean-shock, and wave on wave,
Dash'd on staggering; the sufferer vow'd
In silent agony, that if the ear

Of Heaven would listen, and its arm be strong
To save; upon the first dear spot of earth
Propitious morning shew'd, he would erect
A temple to the Highest. It was heard
(Thus swains relate) the anguish'd vow was heard
Propitious broke the dawn. The winds no more
Swept o'er the madden'd waters, and the voice
Of the great sea-wave died away; scarce heard
Save where the billow chafed the sand and made
Sweet music with the rocks. The welcome Sun
Chasing the tempest, in the brightening East
Victorious rose, and through the scatter'd haze
Brent Tor uplifted his magnific brow,
With shouts tumultuous hail'd!

Brent Tor and its church, c.1890.

What an epic poem! They do not write them like that any more! In fact seamen have made reference to the tor throughout the ages. It has been written that, 'This tor serveth as a mark to sailors who bear with Plymouth haven' and there are many accounts of seamen vowing to build a church if they make land after terrible storms. So maybe I am being too cynical! However the fact remains that the church was built by the monks of Tavistock, as can be proved by dating the remains of the ruined walls of the old abbey seen in the churchyard there alongside those of St Michael of the Rock, Brentor.

The track leads you up some granite steps to a little iron gate and into the churchyard. I am sure you will have paused, not just to get your breath back but to have a look at the marvellous views across the rolling Devon countryside; Dartmoor is on the horizon as is Cornwall and Bodmin Moor with Brown Willy, Plymouth Sound and Whitsand Bay. Look north and you will just make out Exmoor. You are now at 1100ft.

However, there are problems with having a church on an exposed outcrop at over 1000ft. In 1900 Baring-Gould wrote in his *Book of Dartmoor*:

A late curate of Tavistock who took services at Brent Tor and found it often desperate work to scramble to the summit in storm and sleet and rain resolved on forming a roadway. He experienced some difficulty in persuading men to go out from Tavistock, so he supplied himself with several bottles of whiskey and when he saw a sturdy labourer standing idle in the market place he invited him into his lodgings and plied him with hot grog till the man in a moist and smiling condition assented to the proposition that he should give a day to the Brent Tor path.

Richard Polwhele writing in 1800 told of the difficulties the people of the parish of Brent Tor had in getting to church. He wrote:

It has been shrewdly said that the inhabitants of the this parish of Brent Tor... make weekly atonement for their sins; for they can never go to church without the previous penance of climbing up this steep, which they are so often obliged to attempt with the weariest industry and in the lowliest attitude. In windy or rainy weather, the worthy pastor himself is frequently obliged to humble himself upon all fours, preparatory to his being exalted in the pulpit.

There are other splendid stories told by Baring-Gould about the trials and tribulations of climbing up to the church. One stormy, rainy day a man wearing a new blue sweater carrying his baby up to be christened was astonished to discover on arrival at the font that the white christening robes of the child had been turned blue by the dye running from its father's soaked sweater! On another occasion, when mourners and the parson attempted to leave the church in order to go to the grave for a burial they were almost knocked over by a ferocious, howling north-east wind and had to hop like frogs to the graveside. The sexton is supposed to have advised the parson and the party to, 'Crook'y down Sir!' The rest of the service was held in the lee of the gravestones.

One final word of warning: a poor bride slipped on the wet path climbing up to church to be married and ruined her wedding gown. Perhaps it may be better not to get married there, although on a fine day I can imagine no more inspirational place. I hope you do not have any problems!

In spite of Robert Giffard building the church in 1130, with the help of the monks of Tavistock, it was not formally dedicated to St Michael until 4 December 1319 by Bishop Stapledon when the name of the parish was shown as Brente Torre; still more variations of the name. Bishop Bronsecombe who, you will remember, had the slight problem with the Devil and a loaf (Walk 6) mentions it in a deed dated 1269. The walls, which are about 3ft thick, are very low and have a battlemented parapet. They are constructed with volcanic stone taken from the tor itself and green slate from Hurdwick near Tavistock was used as a dressing. The tower is 32ft high and was probably built in the fourteenth century and added to in the fifteenth. The church is only 37ft long and 14ft 6in. wide; it is said to be the fourth smallest parish church in England.

As you wander around outside the church, there are two things to look out for. On the north wall of the church there is an old memorial tablet. It is very worn and covered with lichen but if you look closely you can make out the initials WB and an ornamental border. The writing says, 'HEARE vnder This stone Lyeth the body of walter batten of brinsabach who was bvried April sixth 1677. Allso Alce his wife was bvried the third of desember 1681'. You will remember my mentioning Brinsabach Farm in connection with the Celtic names, so I suppose Walter Batten lived there. If you walk round to the south side of the tower and look up you will see a stone sundial set on the wall. It is said to be one of the oldest in Devon. Although not easy to see, at the top of the dial there is an odd figure wearing a flat cap that seems to be a mixture of an angel and an imp with wings. The name of Walter Batten is at the foot of the dial and initials WB are at the top cutting the date, 1694, in two. The sundial could have been put up as a memorial to the farmer of Brinsabach, Walter Batten, whose relatives were still involved in the work of the church through the ages – a William Batten was the vicar's warden in 1883.

One of the oldest sundials in Devon is set on the wall of the church at Brentor.

Time to go inside now. On your right is a granite octagonal font. Like the font at St Petrock's at Lydford, this font also has the remains of a hinge and staple on the rim, where a lid was once fitted. Holy water was often stolen and used for many purposes including black magic.

Beyond the font to your right the shields of the Giffard family are fixed to the iron gates that lead to the tower. The Giffards have always kept a close interest in the church and in 1969, the 650th anniversary of the dedication to St Michael, one of the lessons in the service was read by Cdr Roger Giffard, a direct descendant of Robert Giffard who built the church.

You will see the bell ropes hanging down at the base of the tower. In 1553 King Edward VI ordered that an inventory should be made of all church goods and Sir Peter Carew carried this royal command out for Brentor. It was recorded that there were two bells and one chalice. These very early bells were made in a local foundry and one of them had the inscription, *Gallus vocor ego, solus per omne sono*, meaning 'I am called the cock and I alone sound above all'. A third

Underneath the lichen this memorial tablet reads: 'HEARE vnder This stone Lyeth the body of walter batten of brinsabach who was bvried April sixth 1677'.

bell was added in the seventeenth century that had inscribed on it 'T.P.I. Colling, W. Nichol, H. Davis Wardens 1668'. In 1909 two more bells were added to make a ring of five with the old bells also being recast in that year. With such a small tower the bells are also fairly small with the heaviest weighing only 6cwt. As with many old churches, bells in old towers need new girders and bearings and these were replaced here in 1958 and 1963.

It is always difficult to find the really old parts of churches when there have been, as is so often the case, so many rebuildings, alterations and additions. Here at St Michael's there are doorways in the north and south walls (unusual features for such a small building) which probably date from the fourteenth century. In the south window the semicircular head could well be twelfth century while the very small and narrow north window shows all the signs of being thirteenth century, although it could even be part of the original church.

The roof is not old, having been replaced in 1889–90 but is said to be an exact copy of a fifteenth-century simple rafter roof. This was all part of the restoration work paid for by Hastings, the Ninth Duke of Bedford at a cost of £729. One rather gruesome and inexplicable find emerged during the work: 40

skeletons were discovered 3ft under the floor. One was lying east to west and the others north to south. Who they were and why they were buried there and placed in such positions is yet to be explained.

It is an awful and disgraceful thing to have to mention but the church of St Michael of the Rock has been subjected to vandalism and theft over the years. The present pastor feels that the church should be open to all at all times and it is therefore never locked. Lead was stolen from the roof in 1951. A pewter flagon was stolen in 1964 and a brass cross and candlesticks were taken in 1969. Recently, in 2002, the central part of the stained-glass window of St Michael, holding the sword of righteousness like a cross and the scales of justice, which was placed in the church in 1971, was smashed and a fire extinguisher let off inside the nave. What is in the minds of such people? Happily the church is so well known and loved by so many people a large sum of money was quickly raised in order to replace the window.

You will be able to buy an excellent little pamphlet about the church of St Michael when you visit, full of detailed information, which indeed I have drawn on here. One of the most interesting and amusing sections concerns the churchwardens' accounts. I quote just a few examples:

1738 Paid a man with a pass yt came from Turkey with his tongue cut out of his mouth.
                                                                                    1s.6d.
1726 Paid for the minister's dinner.   *2s.6d.*
Paid for bread and wine at Christide.   *2s.6d.*
1728 Paid for new bell rope.   *1s.3d.*
Paid for Liquor for ye Rural Dean.   *2s. 6d.*
1748 Paid to John Sloman for oak for floring of the Chancel and the Bellfrey.
                                                                                    £1.6s.6d.
1749 Paid to John Cudlepp for one half Hoghead of cyder.   *10s.6d.*
1791 Susanna Kinsman for Reparing the Hedge an gate.   *2s.6d.*

I like the idea that the liquor for the Dean Rural cost twice as much as a new bell rope! It gives a splendid insight into the expenses of the church and indeed life at that period, especially the burying of the destitute:

Paid for Buring of Jean Fuge, 1758.
The Parson.   *1s.0d*
For the Couffine.   *8s.0d*

A disused pit of the small manganese mine below Brentor.

For Syder.	*5s.2d.*
For a pint of Brandy.	*10d.*
Sope and Candles.	*4d.*
The shrouder.	*3s.6d.*
For making the grave.	*2s.0d.*
For Liquer at ye Servey of Jean Fuge good.	*3s.10d.*

St Michael's is a hard place to leave. 'Nearer to Thee, my God' perhaps! All around is history, legend and fantastic views, on a good day of course!

From the north-west corner of the church look down to the fields below and you will see a small area of woods around what appears to be a quarry. Nothing really to do with the church but this is the remains of a disused pit of a small manganese mine used in the nineteenth century.

Back down to your car; there is a shortcut if you do not want to follow the path made by the 'moist and smiling' labourers from Tavistock.

WALK 9

ROUTRUNDLE, DISUSED RAILWAY TRACK, INGRA TOR, SWELLTOR QUARRIES, KING'S TOR, MERRIVALE PREHISTORIC REMAINS, YELLOWMEADE FARM, FOGGINTOR QUARRIES, LEEDEN TOR.

START: Car park on the north side of the Princetown to Yelverton road (B3212), Walkhampton Common. Map ref.: 561709.
Long. 7.5 miles/12km. Moderate.

This is a long walk if you use the above start and it is one where you could start at the other end by leaving your car in the quarry at the start of the track that leads past Yellowmeade Farm to Foggintor Quarries (map ref.: 567750). Alternatively, it is also possible to walk to one or two of the points of interest from either start if you want just a short evening stroll.

Princetown is about 3 miles away with all the facilities you would expect in a small town with a large, summer, tourist trade.

It is impossible to drive on this part of the moor without being aware of the prison at Princetown; the notorious Dartmoor Prison. However, the story of the building of the prison is not widely known.

Sir Thomas Tyrwhitt, Secretary to the Council of the Prince of Wales and later Lord Warden of the Stannaries, had always had a dream of creating a town in this bleak, high spot, which he would call Princetown in honour of the Duke of Cornwall, Prince of Wales who later became George IV. He planned to turn it into a 'garden city' growing vegetables to sell in Plymouth and to develop a quarry industry nearby. I feel that he had not done his research into Dartmoor weather; growing vegetables high on Dartmoor is not an easy or profitable venture! Nevertheless it was he who laid the foundation stone of a prison here on 20 March 1806, having suggested that this might be a possible location for a penal settlement. It became a prison, for French prisoners captured in the

Entrance gates to Dartmoor Prison, Princetown.

Dartmoor Prison.

Samuel Prout's sketch of the building of Dartmoor Prison, 1807.

war against Napoleon, and by 1812 there were over 9000 prisoners, who lived under terrible conditions with no heating or even glass in the barred windows. Americans were also held at the prison during the War of Independence together with the French. The Latin inscription still seen over the gate takes on a poignant meaning: *Parcere subjectis*, meaning 'Pity the conquered'.

After the Battle of Waterloo in 1815 the prisoners were repatriated and the prison, even though it was used, as I mentioned in Walk 6, as a naphtha factory for a while, was empty for many years and slowly started to fall into decay as did the houses in the town. In 1850, as you may remember from Walk 7, the decision was taken to use the prison for British convicts, including those who would have normally been deported to the colonies, after the closure of the prison at Lydford. The village and the prison of Princetown were revitalised. The hardships for the convicts are difficult to imagine; they spent many hours working in the nearby granite quarries, chained together, and wore clothing marked with broad arrows that I thought was only ever seen in the old, silent, comedy films of Charlie Chaplin!

Over the years myths and legends have grown up around the prison, which is still in use today. The mad axeman getting out at night and drinking in the pub at Mary Tavy is just one! There is a museum just past the entrance to the prison, which is well worth a visit to learn more about the history and the legends.

Life for the inmates is very different in 2002 from that of the early prisoners and attitudes have changed radically over the years; Dartmoor is no longer the prison for the worst offenders. That said, the group of grey, granite buildings with all its associations has a grim, sinister aspect, especially on bleak winter days when Princetown is wreathed in mist.

Guards pose at the forbidding gateway to the prison at Princetown, c.1900.

I shall assume that you will start this walk from the car park on the Princetown to Yelverton road, at Walkhampton Common. You can shorten the walk straightaway if you wish by climbing almost north to Leeden Tor and dropping down the other side but it is more interesting perhaps to set off over open moor in a north-westerly direction down to the **disused railway track** near **Routrundle** Farm. This was once an incredible railway, but was closed in 1956, even before the Beeching axe. If it were still open today it would make an amazing tourist attraction, especially if some enterprising company could run steam trains on the winding, twisting track that contours round the moorland gradually gaining height to Princetown at nearly 1400ft. The views from the railway were superb, as I remember when I rode on it a few months before it closed; one can look out over the moorland and the lowlands to the west of Dartmoor and down into Cornwall and the Cornish moors on the horizon.

The railway started life in 1823 as the Plymouth and Dartmoor Railway that used horse-drawn trucks, as the Haytor granite railway had done (Walk 1) to take granite from the quarries on this walk down to Plymouth. This was all part of the dreams of that Dartmoor industrial pioneer Sir Thomas Tyrwhitt, the builder of the prison. One of his schemes was to establish Princetown as a thriving community by opening quarries on Walkhampton Common, in the first instance, to obtain granite to build the prison. This later developed into five quarries that sent granite down to Plymouth for kerb stones, channels for the drains and huge blocks for the breakwater at the entrance to Plymouth Sound. The horse-drawn trucks ran down as far as the Plym estuary some 25 miles away and not only was the granite used in Plymouth but it also began to be taken by ship to other parts of the country, but more about that later.

The track was eventually taken over by the Great Western Railway in 1883 for steam trains, at which point standard-gauge rails were laid that followed the old route pioneered by the early engineers of Tyrwhitt's tramway. This shows how remarkable the survey for this early route must have been. However, it all ended in 1956. The *Western Morning News* included a headline on 5 March 1956 that read, 'Noisy Funeral of a Railway' at the top of the following article:

Aged seventy-three, the Princetown branch died on Saturday night, when the funeral ceremony was held. Some enthusiasts wore black ties and were suitably mournful for the loss of a friendly little railway; members of the Dartmoor Ramblers' Club marked the occasion by singing 'Auld Lang Syne' on the mist-shrouded platform at Princetown, and afterwards set out to hike to Bellever.

It was a well-attended funeral: 168 passengers used the last public train, the 7pm from Yelverton to Princetown, but hundreds of local people paid their tribute to the line which had served the district so long and so well, in good weather and foul: they waved and cheered as the procession of the two engines and six coaches climbed slowly up across the open moor.

Normally the engine was stationed at Princetown, but all rolling stock was taken off the branch before the gates and points were locked, and passengers who would otherwise have been stranded in the village were allowed to return on the 8.30p.m. special. For forty-five minutes, however they had to stand on the platform, under the uncertain light afforded by the few dangling oil lamps.

There was no light in the waiting-rooms, where the furniture had been removed and the windows boarded up. With the elements unkind, even the keenest enthusiasts were relieved when the train was eventually shunted back to the platform and the last journey began.

Though visibility was only a few yards however, it wound its way round King Tor, stopped at Dousland for a lengthy time while equipment from the station was loaded and people shook hands, and reached Yelverton only about forty-five minutes late.

Only three weeks back the Princetown flier was carrying heavier traffic than normal because road conditions on the moor were tricky. What will happen if there are heavy snowfalls in the years to come is anybody's guess. British Railways say it is not their responsibility. And the branch has after all, been making a loss of £6 for every £1 revenue.

The last passengers have alighted at the diminutive platform at Ingra Tor to read the notice warning them to look out for snakes. Only ghost trains, perhaps carrying the spirit of Sit Thomas Tyrwhitt, will stop at King Tor Halt, the bleakest and (since the last quarrymen left their granite cottages some years ago) the loneliest station in England.

What a sad end.

It is easy, fairly level walking along the old railway track with quite a lot of the ballast remaining. Soon you swing round **Ingra Tor** and back along the hill-side in an easterly direction. You pass quite a few sidings and quarry entrances. The old track goes through a cutting with a bridge over it and then along an embankment and over a bridge with a steam flowing underneath. To your right you can see the horseshoe curve of what was the track for the old horse-drawn trucks which also passes over an ancient bridge before joining our track again.

You are now in an area of enclosures and hut circles, but soon you will notice, on your right, a muddy well-defined track coming down from Leeden Tor (you will be coming down this if you took the first shortcut). This is the track you must follow on the return leg of your journey.

Keep along the old railway track and after a ruined building on your left you can see, to your right, a long, green incline leading up towards some quarries and tower-shaped rocks which form the summit tors of the end of this ridge. This incline, down which were lowered great blocks of granite to the trucks below, is the first part of the **Swelltor Quarries**. It is worth wandering up and spending quite some time exploring this area.

It is possible to scramble and explore where you will but take care for there are some fearful drops! There are a great number of different levels and tracks with the gaunt ruins of various industrial buildings. If you work your way north-west along various levels you will come to several more huge pits all with openings towards the south-west and the railway sidings and inclines below.

As with the granite from Hay Tor (Walk 1) in the nineteenth century a lot of the rock from here was used for buildings in London including Nelson's Column and the old London Bridge. The quarries were working until the late 1930s.

Facing out towards the south-west there are long peninsulas of waste tips like jetties jutting into a sea. The views are marvellous – you can see Cornwall, a corner of the Tamar where it is joined by the Tavy and the railway bridge that goes across to Gunnislake.

At a lower level, if you climb carefully down, you will see the siding or incline that ran north-west towards the main line with many sleepers in position and beside it several more ruined buildings. North-west of the old quarry buildings, on the right of the track you have been following, you will see the large corbels that were cut in 1903 for the widening of London Bridge but were never used; they have lain here ever since. It is odd to think of Dartmoor granite ending up in the United States of America but it is to Arizona that the old London Bridge was taken, bit by bit, in the 1960s. Apparently when the bridge was being dismantled one of the corbels fell and was badly broken. Somebody must have remembered the Swelltor corbels lying here unused, for a lorry was sent from Princetown to pick one up to take to London and then on to Arizona. So granite from Swelltor Quarries and Haytor Quarries now stands in the desert in America; London Bridge is no longer falling down!

Disused and abandoned corbels, Swelltor Quarries.

If you wanted to cut the walk short you could now retrace your steps back along the main track south-east to the bend where there was an obvious bridge over a cutting. Clamber up the steep bank here and head for Leedon Tor almost due south up a long, gentle slope and back down to the start.

However if you want to go further on this walk, then your route runs gently down the incline to the main line which has been below you all the time by the fence. The rocks on your right are King's Tor and soon you can see yet another siding and inclined plane. The track of the old Plymouth and Dartmoor Railway and that of the GWR part company, deviate and join again eventually where there are cuttings, embankments and a bridge. The siding is, in fact, part of the old tramway track. If you follow the track of the Plymouth and Dartmoor Railway out onto the spur, on the bend, you will find three iron clamps for rails still in position from 1823.

The views down the valley of the River Walkham are fine here and you can look across to Longash Common where you are going now. However, if time is short, you can continue round the bend on the disused railway track to **Foggintor Quarries** and cut the walk short by about 0.75 mile. Incidentally, the branch line here leading into Foggintor Quarries was known as the 'Royal Oak Siding' and indeed the name 'Royal Oak' was also in use for the quarry.

The broken capstone of Merrivale's kist, 1895.

If you can, it is certainly worth continuing on this route, so that you can see the prehistoric remains on Long Ash Common – some of the most interesting on Dartmoor and easily accessible from your car if you do not want to do the full walk. From where you are now on the disused railway track, strike north after getting King's Tor dead behind you. You will see the wall of an enclosure ahead. Follow it to the right and cross the stream by the tinners' workings.

North-west of you are prehistoric remains known as the **Merrivale Antiquities**. I suppose Merrivale means 'a pleasant valley', which it is indeed. The Dartmoor Inn is on the road just over the bridge of the River Walkham should you need sustenance.

The menhir at Merrivale, 1889.

The first thing that you will probably notice, away to your left and quite close to the wall that you were following (which has now turned north-west) is a standing stone over 10ft tall called the Longstone (as you will remember from Walk 4, this is a popular name!). The cemetery, for that is what it was, and the other remains lie on the flat plateau of Long Ash Hill and is typical of the sites

The double row of stones at the site of the Merrivale Antiquities.

The kistvaen, also part of the Merrivale Antiquities.

chosen by Bronze-Age man for his monuments. It is an impressive area with kistvaens, stone circles, menhirs, cairns, three stone rows each with blocking stones and even the traces of another stone row. It was known by local people as the 'Plague Market' or 'Potato Market'. In 1625 there was an outbreak of the bubonic plague in Tavistock where there were 575 deaths. In exchange for money local farmers left food on this site for the inhabitants of Tavistock to pick up, so as to avoid any contact between the two groups, thus avoiding further contamination.

From the Longstone, look around to see the slightly flattened stone circle which has a number of granite stones in it which were probably dragged over the moor from King's Tor. Nearby there is a small cairn and a fallen stone over 6ft long. Archaeologists sometimes try to find some reason for the positioning of stone circles and rows. Cardinal-point alignments are found here. The axis of the ring is 88°–268° while the outlying one stands 182° from the centre.

Walk north to the famous 865ft-long double row of stones. Not more than 3ft wide, this would not really be wide enough for a spectacular burial procession. At the western end there is a pillar and a slab while at the eastern end a large triangular stone has been placed firmly across the line as a blocking stone. Nearly halfway down the avenue there is a small circle of seven stones just over 11ft across with a ruined barrow in the middle. Most impressive of all is the magnificent kistvaen standing about 45ft south of the row and about 280ft along from the triangular blocking stone. It is massive: 7ft long, 3ft wide and 3ft 6in. deep. The huge covering slab, as you will see, is in two parts as a stonemason cut it in half for a gatepost in 1860. A flint scraper and a whetstone were found during excavations in the grave but one presumes that anything else would have been robbed years ago.

Further north on the other side of the small stream there is another smaller stone row not lying parallel to the double row but aligned about 2° north. There have been attempts to prove that the rows and the avenues were in some way pointing to the stars of Pleiades or Arcturus or that they were used to predict the moon's phases and even eclipses. None of these theories stick but for whatever purpose they were built the Merrivale Antiquities are fascinating.

Further north are over 20 hut circles in good condition and a large pound with upright stones forming the walls. One final piece of amusing nonsense: you will soon find, without doubt, a large, flat, dressed stone that was probably an unfinished millstone or apple crusher. For years people believed that it was a sacrificial altar of the Druids!

Turn east and walk towards the trees and the walls you can see 300–400yds away. If you keep a little to the south you will see the remains of an old seventeenth-century track with stone markers: 'T' for Tavistock on one face and 'A' for Ashburton on the other.

An unfinished millstone or apple crusher.

When you reach the trees and the ruins (now a car park) you will be at the site of a school built at the start of the First World War on land given by Sir Henry Lopes. It was to be for children who were widely scattered over this area from Rundlestone, Foggintor Quarries and Merrivale and was extremely well built and spacious for the time with the boys and girls having separate entrances and cloakrooms. The floors were wooden parquet blocks while all the classrooms were centrally heated so not only could the children keep warm on cold, wet, bleak moorland days but they could dry their clothes on the hot-water pipes and even keep their pasties warm for lunch! The headmaster, a Mr F.S. Stoyle, had a well-built house that lay behind the main school. Apparently Mr Stoyle, whose wife taught the infants, was the youngest headmaster ever to be appointed in Devon and stayed here for over twenty-one years.

With the school standing in such a high, windswept position there was a constant threat from the weather. Many children had to struggle to get to school through high winds, rain and often deep snow. Mrs Stoyle sometimes had to arrange hot meals and cocoa to warm the children on winter days. Mist and snow were dangerous problems and often the children had to be sent home early. Apparently Mr Stoyle would collect the children in groups according to which direction they had to go in order to get home. He would then produce skipping ropes and with a senior child in the lead the children would head off into the blizzard holding on to the rope, like climbers roped together!

A stone marker inscribed with 'T' for Tavistock.

Deep snow drifts and whooping cough closed the school on several occasions while after one severe winter the water supply froze so there was no central heating. An oil stove was moved into a classroom so that lessons could continue. There were other problems with the water supply when cows trampled on the pipe and broke it. Even with a well dug nearby the supply was still erratic until a pipe was laid from a spring near Foggintor and underground pipes brought a constant flow to the school.

In spite of all the problems and challenges facing Mr and Mrs Stoyle the teaching and general well-being of the children was of the highest order as reports by Her Majesty's Inspectors show. It was a sad day when the school finally closed in 1936 after many of the senior pupils went to the school in Princetown and the Stoyles were left only with infants and mixed juniors. The headmaster's house became a private home with the name 'Four Winds', which is the name now also used for the school itself. Sadly people must have found it difficult to live here because after the Second World War all the buildings gradually fell into decay and the site became derelict. I remember seeing the ruins myself in the 1950s; it looked as though the children had only just left. Although many possibilities were discussed for using the buildings that were so sturdily built, in 1964 the school was demolished and in 1965 the headmaster's house was also pulled down. That was the end of what had been the highest school in England.

The remains of the school at Four Winds.

Walk east beside the road until you come to a pump house on the opposite side. (On your side is the quarry where you could park if you wanted to start the walk from this end or merely do parts of it from here.) On the same side of the road as the pump house is another set of remains of a school once held in the Foggintor Mission Hall. Having been built in 1896 it was not denominational and had a small caretaker's house on one side. The land was given by Sir Massey Lopes and the quarrymen built the little chapel and house; you are still able to see the foundations and a few steps.

The quarrymen's children and those of local farmers and other people living nearby had had very little schooling and it was said that there were over 60 youngsters in the area who were receiving no education at all. It was then suggested that the Mission Hall should be used as a school. The vicar of Walkhampton, the Revd Charles Walker got things going; he agreed to pay a rent of £5 a year, appointed a board of managers, bought desks and other equipment and arranged some alterations in the hall to accommodate the children. On 17 August 1896 the school opened with 41 pupils under the newly engaged mistress Miss Thorne. Very few of the children had ever been to school; only three could read and only a few knew the letters of the alphabet. The rest were, as the Revd Walker put it, 'perfectly untaught'.

Poor Miss Thorne found the same terrible difficulties that the Stoyles were to encounter nearly twenty years later. Children would arrive for school soaked to the skin and had to be sent home again, while some never turned up at all.

The school closed in January 1897, but was reopened again under the stalwart Miss Thorne with an acre for a garden, a playground and a yard. With 60 pupils on the register Miss Thorne left in 1898 even though the HMIs thought that she was doing a good job under the most difficult of conditions. Headteachers came and went until in 1903 under a Mr William Howell there were 95 children and the HMIs complained of overcrowding and the poor condition of the desks. With frequent changes in the headteachers it is no wonder the standards dropped as did the numbers. In 1907 Mr T.R. Addyman arrived and with an assistant teacher and two monitors things looked up for the school with an increase in numbers again. Mr Addyman was quite clearly a strict disciplinarian as entries in the school log-book show:

> George E. – ran away when called and then went to Princetown School to avoid punishment. He decided he wished to return to Foggintor but Mr Addyman refused him entry. When the boy arrived the following week, Mr Addyman, acting on instructions from the Managers, put him across the desk and caned him severely.

Mr Addyman left in 1909 suffering from the after-effects of rheumatic fever and even though the Board of Education kept complaining about the overcrowding (the number of pupils was now 90) the new headteacher, a Mr

Gilbert stayed until 27 September 1912 when the school was closed. It was the promise of the new school at Four Winds that was really the death knell of the Foggintor Mission Hall School. Many of the children would eventually go to school there. One of the last entries in the school log-book reveals children, then and now, are still the same. 'Leonard T. – threw mud and water at Emily S. and swore at Hill Cottages girls. He received several strokes across the thighs and buttocks, and swore at the headmaster and threatened vengeance by his father.' Plus ça change!

From the quarry a rough track runs south which you must now follow. On the right you will see the ruins of what was once a row of cottages called Red Cottages where some of the quarrymen lived. Incidentally, it was from here that the pipe taking water down to the Four Winds school was laid. The track has granite slabs embedded in it with grooves and holes cut in them, which you can see here and there. They were the sleepers for the rails on which ran the horse-drawn trucks that carried some of the granite out to the main road, to be taken away for local use.

Foggintor Quarries.

After a while you pass **Yellowmeade Farm**. On the left, near the farm, you will find another of the ancient, seventeenth-century signposts, like the one near the Merrivale Antiquities, with 'T' for Tavistock and 'A' for Ashburton carved on opposite faces. Soon you arrive at **Foggintor Quarries**, in some ways even more remarkable than Swelltor. On the right there are a great many ruined buildings: remains of what must have been a thriving community that lived a hard life in this remote spot. These were Hill Cottages, built in a square, where more than 30 families lived. Including the workers at the other quarries over 600 men were employed in this industry. The manager's house was well built with bevelled window lintels and a beautiful rose-window. On the right are the long piers of the spoil tips for the waste materials leading out into a tumble of rocks and boulders.

Just north-east of the cottages was a little Wesleyan chapel and yes, you have guessed it, it was used as a school for a while, starting in March 1913 – the year after the Foggintor Mission Hall school closed. Mrs Loop was the mistress and this school proved to be very popular because although it was originally intended for just the 17 infants and juniors, the parents sent all their children, instead of sending the older ones to Princetown! After a lot of discussion with the attendance officer the parents won the day and the senior children were allowed to attend the new school.

Mrs Loop had an uphill struggle trying to keep everything running smoothly in spite of immense difficulties, including getting books and other materials such as blackboards and a stove for the infant's classroom. It all proved too much for her because in October 1913 she had to resign under doctor's orders. Mrs Berger took over and the school was a success with an extremely high attendance record of 99–100 per cent for one month, for which a day's holiday was given. Mrs Berger must have had a thing about cleanliness as the log-book lists many instances of sending dirty children home from school! The school closed on 26 March 1915 and many of the children went on the long walk down to the new school on the Tavistock road, Four Winds.

Enter the quarries on the left by following the narrow cutting. You will then be confronted with an astonishing area of rock walls and deep lakes. As with Swelltor Quarries I find this a fascinating and even beautiful place. I am always astonished at how man can wreak such havoc and destruction by eating away the moorland and leaving ugly pits, yet nature takes over when he has gone and turns a stark, industrial place into something quite beautiful, magical even.

It will not take much imagination to see in your mind's eye what this site must have been like at the height of this thriving industry: many people moving around, quarrymen blasting and hacking at the granite, trucks being loaded to

Above left: *The ruins at Foggintor Quarries.*

Above: *Spoil tips at Foggintor Quarries.*

Disused Foggintor Quarries.

Foggintor Quarries.

start their journeys across the winding, moorland tracks to Plymouth. It is incredible to think that 600 people lived and worked here.

It is sad to think that, only ten years after the opening of the railway, Sir Thomas Tyrwhitt died an impoverished, disappointed and disillusioned man. Although there had been a great many setbacks and failures, he still was the great Dartmoor industrial pioneer and it was his drive and enthusiasm that paved the way for an awakening and understanding of Dartmoor's potential developments with new roads, villages, even Princetown, as well as quarries and other industrial enterprises. It is said that many of the first pioneers and people with vision are those whose 'white bones paved the way for others' feet'.

On leaving this extraordinary place, walk on until you reach the railway track that you left at King's Tor, beyond the last bank of waste materials. Running down to the right is the track that I mentioned just before Swelltor Quarries and you must follow that.

Retrace your route back the way you first came over the bridge across the stream until you come to the cutting with the bridge over it. Climb steeply up to the left and then take the long gentle slope up **Leedon Tor** with its odd-shaped summit rocks. You will pass a reave (an ancient boundary bank) near the top, which is said to stretch as far as Chagford. It is a long way to walk to find out if this is true!

Follow the slight rise heading south and then down past some hut circles to the start of your walk. If it is summer there might be an ice-cream van there!

BURRATOR RESERVOIR, NARRATOR PLANTATION,
SHEEPSTOR VILLAGE, SHEEPS TOR.

START: Near Norsworthy Bridge, Burrator Reservoir.
Map ref.: 568693. Short. 3 miles/5km. Moderate.

There are plenty of places to park your car off the road in this area. Dousland is about 2.5 miles away. Meavy is also quite close with a pleasant pub. There are ice-cream vans parked near the dam of **Burrator Reservoir** at weekends and during the summer. You could just drive round to the village of Sheepstor if that part of this walk interests you but parking is almost impossible there.

From the car parks near Norsworthy Bridge set off along the road close to the edge of the reservoir. You can get glimpses of the pointed Leather Tor that stands like a small mountain on the other side of the lake. Soon you will see to your left where the right of way, marked on the map, enters **Narrator Plantation** just under half a mile from where you left your car. It skirts the forest below Sheepstor on moorland before dropping down to Joey's lane, an ancient packhorse route.

Even though **Sheepstor** was and is a fairly small village it had an importance beyond its size as it was on the Jobbers' Path or as the old moormen called it, the Joblers' Path. The name 'jobber' comes from the wool industry that flourished on the edges of Dartmoor for centuries using the pure moorland streams and rivers for power and washing the wool. A yarn jobber was a man who bought and sold wool and walked his packhorses along the old trackways on Dartmoor when transporting sacks of wool from the farmers down to the mills. The monks at Buckfast, Buckland and Tavistock were Cistercians in medieval times and they were great traders and farmers; they would have used

Sheepstor village, 1891.

Above: *A clapper bridge over Dean Burn on the Abbot's Way, a route once used by the Cistercian monks to carry wool across the moor. The route was also used by the jobbers.*

Right: *Buckfast Abbey.*

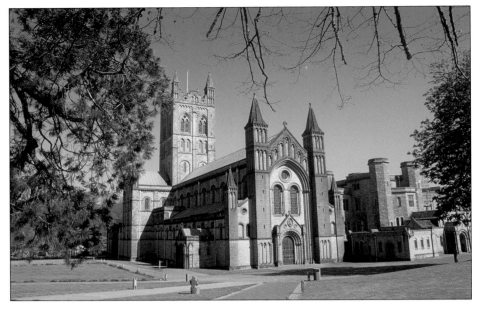

the jobbers to carry their wool. The jobbers would have paused for a few hours and even stayed at Sheepstor before setting out across the wild, open moor to Buckfast Abbey and the mills at Buckfastleigh. There were also a great many farms in this part of Dartmoor where large quantities of wool were produced. The jobbers needed fields and stabling where they could graze and keep their packhorses overnight or for a few days as the farmers brought their wool to them to be transported off the moor to be sold, spun and woven. Sheepstor provided fields and stabling. There was an inn, too, where many stayed and fortified themselves for the long and arduous struggle across the moor.

Turn left along the road at the bottom of the lane and you are almost in the village. The name comes from the tor standing high above the hamlet but nobody is really clear what it means except that it has nothing to do with sheep! It could be a corruption of 'schittes' a medieval word meaning a steep slope or maybe 'scyttel' meaning a bar. In 1168 it was called Sitelestorra, so your guess is as good as mine!

The main feature of Sheepstor hamlet is the lovely little mid-fifteenth-century church, which was built on the site of a much earlier Saxon or Norman church.

There is reference to a chapel in documents of 1280. To enter the churchyard go through the lych-gate near the village cross. Lych or lich is an Old English word for corpse; lych-gates are where a coffin is carried into the churchyard and can be rested on the central platform while the pall bearers pass through on either side and where the mourners can wait before the burial. If you look carefully you will make out the initials W.E. cut in the centre stone; probably those of Walter Elford of Longstone Manor.

The style of the church, as found in many moorland churches, is Perpendicular with granite as the main stone used in the construction. The windows were built using a porphyry quartz which was quarried at Roborough Down near Buckland Abbey. The tower is impressive with large polygonal crocketed pinnacles. It is dedicated to St Leonard, an unusual saint to find on Dartmoor. Apparently he was godson of Clovis, King of the Franks. He became a monk and later went to live in the forest near Limoges, France, as a recluse. By some extraordinary chance the Frankish Queen was near the hermit's retreat deep in the forest when she started to have severe birthing pains.

Sheepstor's Church of St Leonard.

Leonard was able to save her life, and I presume that of her child as well. She was so grateful that she gave him the land around his cell where he later founded a monastery. His main work during his life was ransoming prisoners and he is known as the patron saint of prisoners. St Leonard died in AD560.

When you approach the porch you will see an extraordinary sculpture above the door. Ears of corn sprout out of a skull's eye sockets, while the skull rests on an hourglass. It has been suggested that it symbolises life after death, with the corn representing life and the skull representing death. The hourglass shows that time and life move relentlessly and inexorably on. There are Latin inscriptions around the sculpture. The one below reads: *Mors Janua Vita*, 'Death is the door to life'. Above the inscription reads: *Ut Hora Sic Vita*, 'As the hour so life passes'. On the scroll it says, *Anima Revertet*, 'The soul will return'. There are also the initials J.E. that probably refer to John Elford of Longstone Manor (more of him later).

The lych-gate in the churchyard at Sheepstor.

Inside the church is the beautiful wooden rood-screen. This is not the original fifteenth- or early-sixteenth-century screen because that was ripped out by a Tavistock builder when he was commissioned to carry out restoration work in the 1850s. Apparently it was a magnificent piece of work with gold and coloured paint depicting figures on the panels. However in 1914 the screen was rebuilt on the orders of a far-sighted vicar, the Revd Hugh Breton, following meticulously the architects drawings and even fitting in some of the bits of the original screen that had been saved from the over-zealous builder's destruction. One of the largest surviving pieces can be seen in the right-hand door that leads into the chancel.

On the north wall are three memorials to the Elford family and if you have a moment when you have finished this walk you might like to have a look at the ruins of Longstone Manor which is lapped by the waters of Burrator Reservoir (map ref.: 556695). It stands at the neck of a peninsula that juts out into the lake. This was the home of the Elford family who were the Lords of the Manor. The earliest of the memorials here commemorate John Elford who died in 1684. His wife Elizabeth, commemorated here in the form of an alabaster statue of a reclining lady with a baby beside her, died in childbirth in 1631. There are also three little daughters who are kneeling beside the bed. A poignant monument.

A Pua Kumbu, a ceremonial blanket from Sarawak. It now hangs on the south wall of the church at Sheepstor.

The font is made, as you might expect, of granite with shields and dog-toothed carvings. The scenes carved on the ends of the pews show crusaders alongside castles, a bishop preaching to a king and queen, the signing of the Magna Carta, a sailing ship with its crew and, rather surprisingly here on Dartmoor, the death of St Morwenna within sight of her beloved Welsh mountains.

In the middle of the south wall you will see a ceremonial blanket called a Pua Kumbu that comes from Sarawak, Malaysia. You might well wonder what on earth a beautiful example of native weaving and dyeing is doing in a church on Dartmoor. As you came into the church you will have seen some large panels to your left just inside the door with information about the Brooke family. James Brooke, later Sir James, came from an old Devon family. He was born in India in 1803 while his father Thomas, who was a Judge in the East India Company's Civil Service, was serving in Bengal. He was educated in England but by the age of sixteen he was back in India again, this time, in 1819, as an infantry cadet in the private army run by the East India Company. In 1825 he was wounded in the Burmese Wars. He was taken for dead and handed over to the gravediggers. Luckily a friend noticed that he was still alive and saved him from a terrible death. However his injuries were so severe that he resigned his commission.

When his father died James inherited £30 000, a considerable sum for those days, with which he bought himself a schooner called the *Royalist* and set off in it without any idea where he might end up. In 1839 he had got as far as Singapore where the Governor asked him to sail to Sarawak to take gifts and thanks to Rajah Muda Hassim for the help he had given to some British sailors who had been shipwrecked on the coast there. James surveyed 70 miles of uncharted coast before he sailed up the Sarawak River to be greeted and welcomed by the Rajah Muda Hassim. He had arrived in the middle of a civil war which he helped suppress while travelling along the uncharted coasts and up virtually unknown rivers. It was during this time that he provided help with the country's administration as well as law and order. The people of Sarawak were so impressed with his wisdom and energy that they asked him to become their Rajah. It reads like a *Boy's Own* adventure! On 24 September 1841 he was officially appointed the White Rajah of Sarawak.

Sir James Brooke, 1864.

With a few friends he set about dealing with the piracy and slavery that threatened the coasts, as well as the inter-tribal wars and head-hunting that took place in the jungles inland. This was a country of 50 000 square miles with a population of 300 000 – a mixture of Christians, Chinese, Malays, Moslems. In this country of many different beliefs, religions and attitudes he embraced and respected all the native laws and customs but imposed a British code of justice. He made himself available to anybody who wished to have his advice and help and ruled with sympathy and understanding.

James spent his personal fortune creating the model state, begging for help from the British Government. He never took advantage of his position to make money for himself, indeed he had to borrow money from Baroness Burdett-Coutts when he was penniless. It is said that she was in love with him and even proposed marriage to him on several occasions but James never married.

When he visited England in 1848 Queen Victoria created him a KCB and appointed him Governor of Labuan. In 1852 when Sir James Brooke returned to Sarawak he took with him one of his nephews, Captain John Johnson, son of his sister Emma, who later changed his name to Brooke. James made John his heir and created him Rajah Muda. In 1850 America recognised Sarawak as an independent state but it was not until 1864 that Britain followed suit.

The second White Rajah of Sarawak,
Charles Brooke.

There was another nephew, Charles Johnson, who served twelve years in the Navy and visited Sarawak in 1844. In 1854 he resigned from the Navy and settled in Sarawak having been granted the title of Tuan Muda. Like his brother he also took the name of Brooke. Between them they carried on with the enlightened rule with considerable risk to themselves. In 1857 the Chinese attacked Kuching, the capital of Sarawak. The Rajah escaped by diving into the river, swimming under one of the Chinese ships and disappearing into the darkness. Charles, who had got wind of what was happening, arrived just in the nick of time with a force of loyal Malays and Dyaks. The Chinese retreated in haste and order was restored.

In 1847 the British Government bought what was then Burrator Farm renovated it and presented it to Sir James Brooke for his retirement in recognition of the work he had done in Sarawak. In 1863 after over twenty years as the Rajah, James Brooke finally came to live in what became Burrator House. He obviously loved the place, as extracts from his letters to his nephew Charles reveal, but he was clearly not rich; the British Government had not provided a large pension befitting his extraordinary work in the Far East nor had he amassed a fortune, as he could have done, in the years when he was the first White Rajah.

6 June 1865.
I beg to tell you that your fancy about my being mopish at Burrator is all bosh! I chose the life after mature deliberation, and, aware of the drawbacks within and without, adopted it. There is nothing to regret, for a man cannot elect to have a home of his own, pied-a-terre, and then want what he has not got and cannot afford to get. I resolved to be a country mouse, and can't be a town mouse as well.

I hate society, so called, and I suffer from it. I am fond of Burrator, and won't let you write me out of it. I am as poor as a church mouse and country mouse ought to be, but when we grow richer, and Sarawak has money to spare, I will launch forth into the Italian palace, or villa, or cottage you recommend. I should like to add London chambers, etc., to my refuge at Burrator, and to live as a Rajah should live, clothed in satin raiment and faring sumptuously every day; but till we are richer it is well to be content and happy on what we have.

8 September 1865.
Again I am at my own intent, and enjoying my liberty away from the world and all the world's restraints. This is my Sarawak. I am lord of all I survey, and I try to

make everybody happy. In this, perhaps, consists the secret of contentment when age is stealing from me the joys of physical existence.

There is contentment surely but I also sense a deep feeling of resentment, unhappiness and a longing for the old, adventurous, exciting, pioneering days. James died on 11 June 1868. His nephew John Johnson (Brooke) also died in England in the same year.

Meanwhile in Sarawak his other nephew, Charles, ruled to bring peace and prosperity. He had inherited a considerable national debt and he lived a life of great frugality. In spite of that he brought education to the pirates and head-hunters and gave them schools. He built roads and railways and constructed waterworks, telegraph and telephone systems. While he was there more and more tribes wanted to be included under his rule and the size of the state grew. Like his uncle he carried out all the administration with only a few British assistants and a small force of Sarawak rangers that had been formed in 1846 when the Chinese attacked Kuching. He showed enormous courage, resourcefulness and integrity and won the trust and loyalty of the Sarawak people. He was an austere and autocratic man who tackled problems head on but his radical and visionary views led the way as to how colonial possessions should be ruled.

Sea Dyaks of Sarawak.

In 1888 Queen Victoria created him GCMG and to his delight Sarawak was recognised as a British Protectorate. In 1869 he had married his cousin Margaret de Windt. Sadly their first three children died of cholera but three sons were born and survived; the eldest one continued this extraordinary saga. Aged eighty-eight Sir Charles Brooke died on 17 May 1917 at his home in Cheltenham. He had been the second White Rajah for nearly fifty years.

Charles Vyner de Windt Brooke, the eldest son of Charles the second Rajah, was born in London on 26 September 1874 but was taken to Sarawak as a baby. He was given the title of Rajah Muda at birth but he did not stay in Sarawak during his early days as he went to school at Winchester College in England. As a teenager, quite clearly his future was being planned for him, for he returned to Sarawak to get to know the country and its people and to see his father in action there. After taking a degree at Magdalene College, Cambridge he returned finally to Sarawak aged twenty-three where he joined the Sarawak Service. He embarked on expeditions into the remote parts of the country gaining a fuller understanding of the people and the ways the administration worked. In 1904, aged thirty, Charles junr was left in charge of the country when his father was away and by 1916 he was officially in charge of all the Dyak affairs. In 1917 his father died and immediately he was proclaimed the third Rajah.

Charles junr continued to improve and develop the public works and reformed the legal system. By 1940 the head-hunting and tribal warfare had stopped and at the start of the Second World War Charles was able to give a donation of Sarawak money to Britain for the war effort.

In 1941, the centenary of the founding of the state by Sir James Brooke, Charles set about establishing a Constitution by giving up his own absolute rule as Rajah. When all the details of this were settled he went on leave in Australia but in his absence the Japanese invaded Sarawak and occupied the country. Britain was unable to do anything about this as the war with Germany was at its most difficult and crucial point and the Japanese were moving in on Singapore and Burma. It was a terrible time for Sarawak and Borneo. When liberation came in 1945 Charles did not have the resources to get the country back on its feet and make good the devastation of the occupation. He handed over complete control of Sarawak to Britain and in 1963, after eighteen years as a Crown Colony, the country joined Malaya, Singapore and North Borneo in the Federation of Malaysia.

Charles Vyner de Windt Brooke was created GCMG in 1927 by King George V. He died in London on 9 May 1963, the year that Sarawak joined the Federation of Malaysia, his life work and that of his ancestors finished and accomplished.

The final piece of the saga is Bertram Willes Dayrell Brooke, the second son of Charles, the second White Rajah. He was born in Kuching in 1876 and was granted the title of Tuan Muda by his father at birth. Like his brother, Bertram also attended Winchester College and Cambridge (although he studied at Trinity). He joined the Army and served with the Royal Horse Artillery and was appointed ADC to the Governor of Queensland in 1905.

When his father died in 1917 his brother Charles asked him to resign from the Army and come to Sarawak to help him run the country. Charles made him the Heir Presumptive and left him in charge of the Government when he was away, rather as his father had done for him. He also had the job of presiding over the Sarawak Advisory Council when it met in London at Westminster to discuss the affairs of the Protectorate. He worked well both with and under his brother and had the task of administering Sarawak during the Japanese occupation when his brother was in Australia. On the left of the entrance to the church at Sheepstor there is a memorial to the members of the Sarawak Civil Service who died in Japanese prisoner-of-war camps during the occupation. Bertram showed all the wisdom, understanding and tolerance of his ancestors. His son Antoni was the last Rajah Muda by birth but, of course, he never ruled. Bertram died on 15 September 1965 in Weybridge, Surrey.

The organ in the church was given by Sir Charles Brooke, the second White Rajah. He must have prayed in this church when he came to visit his uncle at Burrator House. Before the organ was built music for the services was provided by the 'Sheepstor fiddlers' who also brought music and dancing to the alehouse where the jobbers drank and stayed. Sheepstor had a reputation for good music.

Outside the church are the tombs of the three White Rajahs of Sarawak. The first, Sir James Brooke, has a massive, square tomb of polished red Aberdeen granite. The tomb of the second Rajah, Sir Charles Brooke, is perhaps more appropriate as it is made of a huge, single slab of granite quarried on Sheepstor. The other tomb in the centre is that of Charles Vyner de Windt Brooke, the third Rajah, which is also made of local granite. Nearby lies the tomb of Bertram Brooke, the Tuan Muda, the Heir Presumptive.

So what else is there to see in this quiet little village which seems to be something of a backwater? Well, there was once a bull-and-bear-baiting arena here; one of many around the moor (the central crossroads in Ashburton are still known as the Bull Ring.) An account of this sport says:

The bull was tied to the ring and then baited with dogs. The dogs which were killed in the fray were usually buried under the stones which supported the ring.

At these barbarous festivities the women wore peculiar leather aprons, in which they caught the bulldog when it was tossed. While a fight was going on, the spectators sat around the churchyard wall and watched the fun, repairing at frequent intervals to the ale-house adjoining the field for refreshment.

The same arenas were also used by wrestlers with bracken being spread over the grass to make a sort of matting to ease the falls. They wore special wrestling

The window at Sheepstor's Church of St Leonard, commemorating the lives of those lost in Sarawak during the Second World War.

The tomb of Sir James Brooke.

clothing of worsted stockings, breeches and a short linen jacket which was the only part that could be used for a hold or hitch. This type of garment is still seen today being used by Cornish and Breton wrestlers. Finally they wore shoes soaked in bullock's blood – I have no idea why! To give you some idea of what it was like at these wrestling bouts, our old friend the Revd John Swete provides an explanation. He went to a Fair at Two Bridges where he observed that, 'The women had in a great measure withdrawn; and the amusements of the men seem'd to be confined to wrestling and drinking'. By the way, in case you are hoping to find the alehouse open I am afraid that the village hall has been built where it once stood.

Along the lane from the churchyard and just around the corner is St Leonard's Well, set into the wall to your left. It is said that the spring has never failed and there is mention of the well in a deed of 1570. The carved canopy over it was taken from the east window of the church during the restoration in the 1850s, presumably at the same time the rood-screen was destroyed by the builder.

Continue along the lane towards the south-east until you come to the first turning left. Follow this past Lamb's Park and soon you will emerge on to open moorland with the rocks of **Sheeps Tor** rising up above you to the left. If you wanted just to wander up to the rocks of the tor then it is possible to drive here; there are places to park without blocking the lane.

It is quite a steep climb up Sheeps Tor and on your way up, to your left, you might be able to find the small chamber formed by the rocks called the Pixies Cave or the Piskies House. Many years ago it was possible to get several people into this cleft but the rocks have shifted and it has almost disappeared. Legend has it that, during the Civil War, a member of the Elford family was supposed to have hidden in the cave when being hunted by the Roundheads. There were stories of paintings on the walls that were said to be the work of the hidden Elford. There are also several pixie stories told about the cave and as this is Dartmoor I am sure you will believe them too!

Sheepstor village.

The south-east rock-face of the tor has quite a number of climbs on it and you may well see outdoor education groups using it. At the foot you should be able to find the remains of a granite vermin trap; made of granite slabs this trap had a funnel-shaped entrance with an ingenious trip-catch system that

The dam at Burrator under construction, 1898.

Construction of a suspension bridge over the reservoir at Burrator, 1925.

caused a slate to drop down to imprison the likes of stoats and weasels. If you clamber round to the summit, taking great care for the drops to the south-east are lethal, you should find another trap.

From the top the views are some of the best on Dartmoor. Below to the north-west is Burrator Reservoir which, in spite of what the critics of man-made lakes say, is one of the most beautiful settings in Britain. You can look out over the moors to Gutter Tor and beyond, while to the west and north-west you can see the Cornish moors.

You may notice on the 1:25 000 maps that Feather Bed is printed on the area of Sheeps Tor. This refers to flat pavements of exposed granite found usually on the summits of high ground on Dartmoor (which you might also have noticed down in Joey's Lane, if you came that way to Sheepstor hamlet).

One possible route back to your car takes you down to Maiden Tor, a low out-crop on the flank of the main tor where there are some Pillow Mounds. These are the artificial burrows made for rabbits by the old warreners who bred them commercially, hence the vermin traps mentioned above. There will be more about that in the next walk. After the Pillow Mounds join the path below you that you used at the beginning of the walk. As an alternative route drop straight down from the summit, north to Narrator Plantation and the ruins of Narrator Farm, to reach the road where you turn right to get back to your car.

WALK 11

NORSWORTHY BRIDGE, DEANCOMBE FARM, CUCKOO ROCK, POTATO CAVE, EYLESBARROW MINE,
NUN'S CROSS FARM, SIWARD'S CROSS, STONE ROW, DOWN TOR.

START: Near Norsworthy Bridge, Burrator Reservoir.
Map ref.: 568693. Medium. 7.75 miles/9.3 km. Moderate.

There are plenty of places to park your car off the road in this popular area. Dousland is about 2.5 miles away. Meavy is also quite close with a pleasant pub. There are ice-cream vans parked near the dam of the reservoir at weekends and during the summer.

If you park at *Norsworthy Bridge*, you will see the road round the reservoir begin to swing south and an obvious track that runs along the edge of the forestry plantations in a south-easterly direction. This is the track you must follow. It is easy walking with pleasant glimpses into the forest with mature trees, mainly conifers. However, there are quite a number of gnarled beeches growing on the mossy banks to your left.

You pass some old, ruined mine buildings set in a dell on your right and then ahead, up a rocky lane you will see the ruins of *Deancombe Farm*. Just before the farm a 'stroll' comes down from Down Tor which you might like to find and follow for your return. Stroll is the name given to the funnel-shaped walls that lead down off open moorland that were used when collecting and driving animals to the lower fields. With ponies this herding is known as the 'pony drift'.

Deancombe Farm in 1935.

Being a romantic at heart I always feel sad at the sight of these old moorland farms; in our difficult world they were not possible to run, so now represent a dim and distant way of living. This is still an idyllic place and until a few years ago the outbuildings and the house itself were easy to see. It must have

Above: *Disused mine buildings along the track that leads to Deancombe from the car park.*

Above right: *Moss-covered walls at Deancombe Farm.*

Straddles among the ruins of Deancombe Farm.

been quite an important place for it is on a crossways of tracks with another stroll leading down to Deancombe Ford.

The site was known as Dannicombe until Victorian times, although in 1317 it was recorded as Denecomb. This was a venville and the fifteenth-century accounts of the Forester of the West Quarter states that, 'the vill of Dennecumbe in the parish of Walkhampton paying a venville rent of 1s.6d.'

On your left in what was the farm court there are a series of granite blocks or straddles that were part of a rick bed to keep the corn or hay dry, off the ground and away from vermin. All around in the ruins are massive granite blocks, posts and lintels and one wonders at the ingenuity and resourcefulness of these early farmers in cutting, dressing and transporting granite.

Go on through the farmyard on the track and you see **Cuckoo Rock** standing ahead of you. Walk through the fields and out to open moor. Hop across the stream and follow the path that climbs quite steeply up to Cuckoo Rock. I suppose it looks a little like a young, gaping cuckoo waiting to be fed by its foster parents. Or maybe this corner is a favourite haunt of cuckoos.

There used to be a Dartmoor letter-box on the summit of the rock but as the climb and descent were dangerous it has been removed. There was sometimes a letter-box hidden in the large cavity at the base of this rock column which is similar to the Bowerman's Nose near Manaton but as this is a popular and easy place to reach it was often vandalised. Much more interesting is the fact that this cavity is said to have been where smuggled liquor was frequently hidden!

Aim diagonally down across the hill, following a fairly obvious path but if you cannot find it aim at the clump of trees in the valley. When you get there you will be at the ruins of Combeshead Farm, another place of ghosts. Once again it is possible to see how well these old farms were built. In 1932 William Pengelly died here aged ninety and was taken on a wagon past Cuckoo Rock, Deancombe Farm and along Nelder's Lane to be buried in Sheepstor church-yard. It was only after the Second World War that the farm became deserted and was left to decay into the ruins you can see today.

Above: *Cuckoo Rock.*

Left: *The ruins of Combeshead Farm with Cuckoo Rock beyond.*

Combeshead Farm, 1934.

Walk through the old farm gates and after a short distance look for a path that runs uphill for 200yds or so past some walls on the bracken-covered slope. Follow this path and in a low, walled bank you will find a small entrance to the **Potato Cave**. It is quite snug and dry inside and you could shelter from the rain if you get

Above: *The interior of the Potato Cave, 1890.*

Right: *The Potato Cave at Combeshead Farm.*

caught out. This is where the farmer from Combeshead kept his crop of potatoes dry and at an even temperature (although the original cave might have been made by the tinners from the workings above). There is also a suggestion that various caves in this area were made for illicit stills and the storage of contraband liquor.

Drop back down to the track and turn left down to the Narrator Brook. You should be able to cross the stream here either by the ford or on the footbridge. Follow the path as it strikes uphill and slightly left until you see a trench or gully on your right, part of the tinners' workings. Leave the path and follow the gully in for a short distance and you will see a low entrance in the hillside. It is usually a little wet but if you duck down you can get into the small chamber and once inside you are able to stand up. The walls are well constructed in stone and it has a conical, beehive-style roof. It could have been made by the tinners to store their picks and shovels and even their tin ingots but I prefer the more romantic idea that this was also a place to hide an illicit still or smuggled goods brought up from the coast. During the eighteenth century there was much smuggling along the Channel coast and there are many stories of contraband being carried up to Dartmoor by packhorse and hidden by the moormen and tinners. I am sure the thirsty work of mining and smelting made the tinners only too glad to have a little extra in the way of liquor, especially if it was smuggled and cheap! It would be a brave, even foolhardy, exciseman who would venture on to the moors to confront the tough tinners with accusations of drinking either bootleg or contraband liquor. No doubt the moormen and the tinners were not the only groups involved in this practice:

Five and twenty ponies trotting through the dark,
Brandy for the Parson, baccy for the Clerk.
Laces for a lady, letters for a spy.
Them that asks no questions isn't told a lie.
Watch the wall, my darling, while the Gentlemen go by!

Watch your head as you come out of the cache and then climb up the rest of the hill until you are on more level ground. Walk south-east and you will find yourself in what was an area of intensive tin streaming and digging from medieval times. Soon you will see evidence of the workings connected with the ***Eylesbarrow Mine*** of the eighteenth and nineteenth centuries. There is an adit marked on the 1:25 000 maps and you will find a low entrance at the head of a gert (tinners' gully) with a stream running out of it. The walls and roof are extremely well built with stone.

Higher up, at the head of a marshy area by a wheel pit and at the end of the line of twin stones that held the flat rods, there is a low, wet entrance to another tunnel: the Two Brothers adit. These workings may collapse, so I would not recommend your entering more than a few feet.

The entrance to an adit at Eylesbarrow Mine.

Keep walking east towards Eylesbarrow Mine. If you do not arrive straight at the mine you will probably reach a track that runs west down to Scout Hut. Eylesbarrow Mine lies on this track. The first reference to this area comes in 1671 when the site was called Yelsborrow but most of the mine workings you see date from around 1815. From then until the second half of the nineteenth century the mine had several different names including Eylesbarrow, Dartmoor Consols and during the last years until 1852, Wheal Ruth. The main company was Dartmoor Consolidated Mines, which was largely funded by Sir Ralph Lopes who let out the land for mining in 1814. It was a thriving village with nearly 100 men working on site.

The most prosperous time for the mine was the 1820s; it even had its own smelting house, the remains of which is down the track towards the south-west, where the valley runs through to Drizzle Combe on the left. There were seven stamping mills, six of which were near the largest water-wheel, built in 1847, which had a leat that took water from the River Plym. The miners knew this as New Engine Leat. You can still make out traces of it running round Hartor Hill to a large collecting pond on the hillside above the mine. There were several other wheels and wheel-pits for working the stamping mills and pumps.

You will have seen already the pairs of stones with grooves cut in the top. There are several more to be seen uphill from the main ruins. This was a method of using iron flat rods that were pushed backwards and forwards on a steel axle lying across the stones in the grooves. One of the runs of the flat rods was over 1200yds from the main wheel; what a sight it must have been.

Above: *The ruins of Eylesbarrow Mine.*

Above right: *Pairs of stones for the flat rods.*

If you have time walk down Hooper's Valley to Plym Ford for there are ruins to see down there, including a building that stored the powder for blasting as well as a smithy and a counting-house.

There were many more people living and working in these remote places than there are today. Not all the miners lived full-time in the barracks and many would walk to work daily from Walkhampton, Sheepstor and Meavy. In the early 1820s the output at Eylesbarrow rose from 107 blocks of tin in 1824, to 403 blocks in 1825. By 1832 output dropped and in 1841 just three or four men were employed and only the mine captain, Mr T. Gregory, and his family lived there.

In 1844 all mining stopped but by 1845 a new company, The Dartmoor Consols Tin Mining Company, had taken over and the mine opened up again. For a few years all seems to have gone well until 1848 when financial difficulties appeared and once again the mine was sold. By 1850 there were new owners and the mine was known as Wheal Ruth. The year 1851 saw production stopping and starting and by 1852 only two miners were employed until on 30 September the mine was closed forever and all the equipment sold by auction.

One of the mine captains, a Mr J.H. Deacon, who had also been the company's chairman, went on living in the captain's house, which was known as the mansion, for quite a few years after the mine had closed. Once he left, the mansion and all the other mine buildings began to decay as slowly nature took over and softened the ruins of this industrial enterprise that opened with the work of young men who might have been veterans of the armies that vanquished Napoleon. A sad end to a Dartmoor industry after just under fifty years.

Ruins at Eylesbarrow, 1889.

Follow the track north-east and then north past deep pits and flat-rod stones. You might like to walk up to the burial cairns on the summit of Eylesbarrow; these are the barrows from which comes the name. From here there are panoramic views of large areas of Dartmoor and the lowlands to the west. You can follow the boundary stones towards the north or if you did not climb up to the cairns then the track will lead you round and down towards the north. This track is something of an eyesore as it has been designed to take mountain bikes; from *Nun's Cross Farm*, where you are heading, it is an unsightly feature running across the hillside. Walk downhill to the building which you will soon see.

This empty farm is typical of a fairly modern newtake (reclaiming and enclosing fields from open moorland) and you can see the fields around the building that were enclosed by a John Hooper in 1870. The building there now replaced a little, thatched croft that he first built on his land. There was a tradition that if you could build a dwelling and have a fire

Nun's Cross Farm.

burning in the hearth within 24 hours you could claim the land around it. I am not sure as to the truth of this!

A few years ago Nun's Cross Farm was derelict and had been badly vandalised. It is a Duchy of Cornwall property and I am glad to say that it has been repaired and is sometimes used now as a training base for youth adventure courses. If you walk straight down to the farmhouse you will see the tunnel of the Devonport Leat. It is worth wandering back down towards the south-east from the farm, following a track along the line of a wall to where the leat flows into the entrance of a tunnel. You may be amused to see that there is a notice on the grill guarding the entrance with a warning of radon gas within the tunnel. Most of the old farms on Dartmoor are now and have always been full of radon gas; it is one of the hazards of living on granite! You may see small brown trout flitting about in the peaty water in the leat, full of radon gas too, of course. It is an amazing feat of engineering, for the whole leat (which starts on the Cowsic River, north of Princetown) and this tunnel were built in the 1790s. It contours round the hillsides so that the flow is gradual and slow. Before Burrator Reservoir was built the leat took water to Devonport, in Plymouth, for the Navy and the ships there. Lower, disused sections of this leat and a much earlier one called Drake's Leat, built in the 1580s by Sir Francis Drake for his galleons and their crews, can still be seen running almost to the outskirts of Plymouth on Roborough Down. Devonport Leat now flows into Burrator Reservoir so it still helps to provide Plymouth with water, as Drake's Leat did for nearly three centuries. Much of the leat was built by French prisoners of war held at Princetown and what an extraordinary job they made of it with it's granite walls still in position and holding the water back after more than two hundred years.

Return to the farm and walk north-west across the field to the tall cross that you can see standing by a broken wall. This is Nun's Cross or **Siward's Cross**. It is one of the earliest crosses on Dartmoor and was mentioned in 1240 as a boundary marker of the Forest of Dartmoor in the perambulation of that year. You may remember that the Longstone on Shovel Down (Walk 4) on the far side of the moor was also one of these markers. It is possible that this cross was put up in the time of Edward the Confessor when Siward, Earl of Northumberland held the manors of Tavei and Wifleurde. If you look carefully you can just make out his name carved on the east side of the cross. On the other side, the words 'Boc Lond' are carved, which must refer to Buckland; this was probably carved by the monks of Buckland Abbey whose lands

Nun's Cross, 1895.

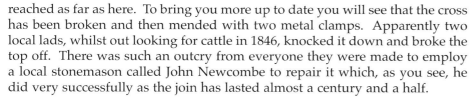

Left: *Nun's Cross or Siward's Cross.*

Above: *It is just possible to make out the carving on the east face of Nun's Cross, which is thought to have been erected at the time of Edward the Confessor (c.1003–66).*

reached as far as here. To bring you more up to date you will see that the cross has been broken and then mended with two metal clamps. Apparently two local lads, whilst out looking for cattle in 1846, knocked it down and broke the top off. There was such an outcry from everyone they were made to employ a local stonemason called John Newcombe to repair it which, as you see, he did very successfully as the join has lasted almost a century and a half.

One final word about the name. Nun could well be a corruption of the Celtic word 'nans' meaning a valley or dale; it was named Nannecross in records dated 1699.

From the cross walk west and you will find the gully where the Devonport Leat flows out of the tunnel. There is a little ruin, just north-west of the exit, which was probably a tinners' shelter with a good fireplace still in position. Keep to the left bank of the leat for a while and then strike out north-west across the hillside. It is quite awkward going with a lot of heather and grass tussocks to wade through. There are some interesting hut circles and enclosures to look at on your way. After a while you will see another enclosure and a cairn for which you should aim. This will bring you to one of Dartmoor's finest **stone rows** with a stone circle at its west end. It has been suggested that the shadows at sunrise of the largest stones predicted the summer solstice.

Above: *Restoration at Down Tor stone row, 1894.*

Right: *The Down Tor stone row and circle.*

When you arrive at the north-east end of the row you will see a large terminal stone about 5ft high which stands at right angles to the main row which climbs in a slight curve up the hill for 340yds to the circle. This circle consists of some 25 stones placed a ring around a low cairn that has been ransacked and robbed at an earlier date. This may have occurred in 1880 when the whole site was ransacked. The largest stone at the east end of the row is nearly 10ft high and weighs about 5 tons. It needed twenty-four workers with a sort of hoist to get it upright again in 1884 after it had been knocked down.

In an almost westerly direction, **Down Tor** lies ahead. It is a gentle walk across to the rocks and then from the tor, follow an obvious, well-worn path through the fields of the old farms of Deancombe and Narrator. This will lead you back down to the start, at Norsworthy Bridge.

Alternatively, you might like to drop due south from Down Tor past a small cairn and some hut circles to find the funnel-shaped walls of the stroll that will lead you back down to the ruins of Deancombe Farm. The 1:25 000 map shows this stroll very clearly. Once back at the bottom turn right and follow the track that you came out on to return to your car.

WALK 12

DITSWORTHY WARREN HOUSE, DRIZZLE COMBE ANTIQUITIES,
GIANT'S BASIN, SCOUT HUT.

START: Burcombe Ford on Sheepstor Brook. Map ref.: 579673.
Route A: Medium. 3 miles/5km. Easy.
Route B: Short. 2.5 miles/4km. Easy.

Meavy is the nearest village (about 2.5 miles away) with a pleasant pub and a Post Office stores. Alternatively, use Dousland or Yelverton.

Follow a broad rough track, known as Edward's Path, that sets out south-east below Gutter Tor. Although I cannot discover the identity of Edward, it seems this path was cut to link up farms, mines and villages. The map shows Edward's Path as a right of way running across the open moor to the east of the track. The name Gutter is unusual. The name is supposedly linked to the fact that goats once grazed here. It seems more likely that the site was originally called Cut Tor because there is quite a large cleft on the tor. However, as this is Dartmoor it is not surprising that we have other possibilities! It could be that the name is linked to the existence of a leat built by tinners that ran from near the tor; they used the word gutter to mean leat. It was shown as Gotetorre in the Assize Rolls of 1281 and 1317 and Gotterknap in a deed of 1539! Just to add to the confusion wild cats are also said to have lived, bred and hunted here.

Follow Edward's Path, keeping an eye out for a vermin trap and the remains of an old longhouse. Soon you will pass many of the artificial burrows of **Ditsworthy Warren House**. This is one of many Warren Houses on Dartmoor where rabbits were

Artificial rabbit burrows near Ditsworthy Warren House.

bred commercially and you can see many of these artificial burrows as you approach the house.

Ditsworthy Warren House.

A stone dog kennel in the kennel court at Ditsworthy Warren House.

Although nobody lives here permanently the house is in quite good order with the windows and doors shuttered. As with Nun's Cross Farm (Walk 11) it is used by youth groups as a base for adventure training at certain times of the year. The small enclosed grass area in front of the house with a stream flowing through is a quiet and peaceful place when the youth groups are not there! To the east of the house there is a walled yard or paddock where the warreners kept their dogs that were used to drive the rabbits into the nets. It is known as a kennel court and you can see several stone kennels cut into the granite walls. It is said that the dogs were so vicious that the warreners had to stand on the walls to throw them their food rather than entering the enclosure!

Apparently this farm was used for warrening until the 1950s when the Rabbit Clearance Order was introduced and it became illegal to farm rabbits in this way; yet another Dartmoor industry brought to an end after centuries. Rabbits were introduced into Britain in the twelfth century and some of the Warren Houses, such as Trowlesworthy Warren, date back to 1272. Wild rabbits' meat was sold in Plymouth and some was even transported up to the Midlands, while the skins made clothing and gloves. You may remember that rabbit bones were found during the excavations at Okehampton Castle (Walk 5)

Take the track behind the Warren House towards the north-east. In wet weather there may be a few marshy areas to navigate but soon you will see several splendid stone rows in an area called **Drizzle Combe,** which is a corruption of Thrushelcombe. I know I have declared most of the stone rows and circles we have visited on previous walks as being among the best on Dartmoor but now we have come to *the* best! The antiquities at Drizzle Combe are the most amazing and fascinating arrangement of stone circles, long rows, standing stones, kists, cairns and pounds in Western Europe. On this site you can really feel the atmosphere of the early Bronze-Age people who built this extraordinary complex. To the west of the stones there is a large crowded settlement of hut circles on Whittenknowles Rocks, and to the north-east there are more pounds and huts at the ends of the rows.

R. Hansford Worth, one of the great Dartmoor antiquarians, whose book is listed in the bibliography, mentioned in a paper that he read at a meeting of the Plymouth Institution in 1889 that he had noticed that several of the tallest and finest of the menhirs in this area, were lying on the ground. As a result of this Worth made arrangements for them to be put up again in the summer of 1893 and these are the ones you see today, along with all the others that were still in place. While they lay on the ground Worth measured them and found that the three largest were 17ft 10ins, and 4ft wide at the base, and probably weighed 7 tons. The others were 12ft 6in. by 9ft 5in. Even with part of them buried in the earth to keep them upright, as they are now, the largest standing stone is about 14ft high and is the tallest menhir on Dartmoor. It lies as the terminal stone of a row that is 296ft long, while the cairn circle at the other end is small but similar to the stone circle at the Down Tor circle (Walk 11). There are two other rows, each with large terminal stones that Worth measured. They have cairn circles at the opposite ends to the terminal stone. Nowhere else on Dartmoor are there such massive terminal stones at the ends of rows.

Also in the area are two great cairns, one of which is called the **Giant's Basin**. It lies quite close to the barrow where the first and longest row ends. The centre has been hollowed out and forms an enormous depression. Nobody is quite sure what its purpose was nor indeed if it was linked to the main building period of the stone rows and menhirs but it does seem likely to be connected.

It is worth spending quite a bit of time wandering around as there are so many Bronze-Age relics to see. As well as the incredible stone rows there are three kistvaens, one of which is an excellent example although it has been

The menhir at Drizzle Combe, 1894.

One of the stone rows at Drizzle Combe.

The tallest menhir on Dartmoor.

The Giant's Basin and stone row, Drizzle Combe.

plundered as the stone lid has been pushed aside. There are also pounds and hut circles to the north-east of the stone rows.

So what was it all about? The alignment of the row with the tallest terminal stone is quite close to the most northerly rising of the moon but there is a possible mathematical reason for the overall shape of the complex. There appears to be a sort of unexpected symmetry. The positioning of the cairns, rows and terminal stones produces an enormous trapezoid. It is unclear as to the significance of this but it suggests that all the cairns, stone rows, barrows and other Bronze-Age relics on Dartmoor were not erected haphazardly; there must have been some purpose behind them whether it was ceremonial, ritual or astronomical. I doubt if we shall ever know for sure, but it is fun to speculate.

Time for decisions now: Route A or Route B.

Route A, the slightly longer one, takes you back up the lovely, shallow valley of the stream of Drizzle Combe towards the north-north-east. You pass another kist and then just before you meet the track that runs down from Eylesbarrow Mine you will see the ruins of the Eylesbarrow mining activities. You could include Eylesbarrow Mine in this walk and look at all the details given in Walk 11. Alternatively, turn left down the track that will lead you to the Scout Hut and your car.

Route B will take you up to the moorland of Whittenknowles Rocks, having hopped across a few streams, to look at the enclosed settlement of hut circles where surely the builders of the stone rows lived. This is another place that makes the hair rise up on the back of my neck if I sit and think about these ancient people! With another hop or two across a leat you will find the track that is marked incorrectly as Edward's Path on the map which will lead you to the Scout Hut and so to your car.

EPILOGUE

Throughout this book we have walked into the history of the Stone Age, the Bronze Age and the Iron Age. We have seen something of the life of the Anglo-Saxons and the Normans. Medieval farmers and tinners lived and worked on Dartmoor and we have walked their ways. In addition, Victorian entrepreneurs and founders of the Empire have all contributed to our understanding of the history of Dartmoor. Much more could have been written and discovered as we have only touched the surface of what there is to be found in this rich and varied corner of Britain.

Dartmoor ponies, the emblem of Dartmoor National Park.

BIBLIOGRAPHY

Archaeology of the Devon Landscape, produced by Dartmoor National Park Authority.

Archaeology of Dartmoor from the Air, published by Devon Books in association with Dartmoor National Park Authority.

Burl, Aubrey. *A Guide to the Stone Circles of Britain, Ireland and Britain.*

Crossing, William. *The Ancient Stone Crosses of Dartmoor and its Borderland.*

Crossing, William. *Guide to Dartmoor.*

Crossing, William. *A Hundred Years on Dartmoor.*

Crossing, William. *Amid Devonia's Alps, or Wanderings and Adventures on Dartmoor.*

Crossing, William. *Gems in a Granite Setting.*

Crossing, William. *A Dartmoor Worker.*

Gill, Crispin.(ed). *Dartmoor; A New Study.*

Harris, Helen. *Industrial Archaeology of Dartmoor.*

Harvey, L.A. & St Leger-Gordon, D. *Dartmoor.*

Hemery, Eric. *High Dartmoor.*

Hoskins, W.G. *Devon.*

Langmuir, Eric. *Mountaincraft and Leadership.*

Perkins, John. *Geology Explained: Dartmoor and the Tamar Valley.*

Pettit, Paul. *Prehistoric Dartmoor.*

Stanbrook, Mary. *Old Dartmoor Schools Remembered.*

Worth, R. Hansford. *Dartmoor.*

Photograph credits:
Burnard Collection (courtesy The Dartmoor Trust) pages 13, 24, 26, 30, 31, 50, 51, 57, 58, 63, 69, 81, 94, 95, 107, 115, 130, 133, 134, 136.
Taylor Collection (courtesy Dartmoor national Park Authority) pages 126, 127.
Pauline Hamilton-Leggett (from her book *Emma and the White Rajahs of Dartmoor)* pages 119, 120, 121, 123.
Other photographs are from the author's collection.